A Gay Republican Challenges Politics as Usual

Richard Tafel

SIMON & SCHUSTER

SIMON & SCHUSTER
Rockefeller Center
1230 Avenue of the Americas
New York, NY 10020

SIMON & SCHUSTER and colophon are
registered trademarks of Simon & Schuster, Inc.

Designed by Ruth Lee

Manufactured in the United States of America

1 3 5 7 9 10 8 6 4 2

Library of Congress Cataloging-in-Publication Data

Tafel, Richard.
Party crasher : a gay Republican challenges politics as usual /
Richard Tafel.
p. cm.
Includes index.
1. Tafel, Richard. 2. Politicians—United States—Biography.
3. Gay politicians—United States—Biography. 4. United States—
Politics and government—1989– 5. Republican Party (U.S. : 1854–)
—Biography. 6. Gay rights—United States. I. Title.
E840.8.T34 1999
305.9′0664′092—dc21
[b]   99-19345
CIP

ISBN 0-684-83764-1

ACKNOWLEDGMENTS

I'D LIKE TO ACKNOWL-
edge Kevin Ivers, who has been my right hand in all of my
political efforts. I couldn't have produced this book without
his thoughts and editing help. I'd also like to acknowledge
Jed Mattes, my literary agent—this book was his brainchild.
I'd like to thank Peter J. Gomes, my mentor, for his insights
and criticisms of my earlier drafts. And I'd like to thank my
editor, Chuck Adams, whose thoughtful insights really made
this book the best that it could be.

To my parents,
who taught me the values of honesty and faith,
even if they didn't know exactly where
those values would take me.

CONTENTS

PROLOGUE

I WAS SITTING AT THE bar at Oil Can Harry's in Austin, Texas, enjoying a night out with the board of directors of the Log Cabin Republicans, when I was approached by a friendly Texan who naturally asked me, "So what brings you to Texas?"

"I'm here with the Log Cabin Republicans board meeting," I responded.

"Oh." He rolled his eyes, thought for a minute, and asked with a grimace, "You're not with that guy Rich Tafel, are you?"

"Well, actually, I am. Why do you ask?" I said.

"He's just such a racist. He's self-hating in that Republican Party. He hates drag queens and is always sucking up to the religious right too. He's just using the gay community to get himself some tax cuts, and wants to make sure he doesn't have to share his money with anyone else, especially not the poor."

As he was speaking, all that I could think of was how untrue this stranger's stereotypes and misguided accusations were.

During my appearance on conservative columnist Armstrong Williams's TV program, *The Right Side*, Williams portrayed gay men in general, and myself in particular, as wanting to have sex with young children. He even went so far as to imply that by my having brought my partner into my parents' home, I had disgraced my family and brought my sin upon them. It was one of the worst debates I had ever been a part of. During one of the breaks, a male show staffer came out to apologize to me. But Williams leaned over to me and asked, "Ever slept with a girl?"

When I shook my head no, he shot back, "Well that's all ya need."

Tired of being nice, I asked, "Armstrong, ever been with a guy?"

He jumped out of his chair with dramatic signs of disgust. I just couldn't wait for the whole thing to be over. Some time later, Armstrong was accused of sexually harassing a male member of his staff.

These two encounters in some ways serve as a metaphor for the work of a gay Republican. I've been demonized and been called names by those on the right who have never taken the opportunity to get to know me. And I've been caricatured and demonized by those on the gay left who also would rather despise what they think I am than find out who I really am. The insistence from both sides that they just want tolerance and respect for their side just doesn't ring true.

How did a nice guy like me find myself caught in the crossfire of American politics? Well, I certainly didn't grow up dreaming about being a gay activist. I actually wanted to be a minister. My background is very unlike that of most political types in Washington. This really hit home when I read Ralph Reed's book *Active Faith*. First, I was struck by the fact that the book had nothing to do with faith, but I also took note of his biography, with his emphasis on getting involved with politics early in life. Because we are roughly the same age, I could look at each year of his life and remember exactly what I was doing then. I found a perverse parallel.

While Reed talked about early campaigns he volunteered for, I remembered my life revolving around the church. I can still remember that Monday was Fellowship of Christian Athletes, Wednesday was Bible Study, Thursday was Junior Choir, Sunday began with Sunday School, then church, followed by Youth Fellowship at night; in all of these groups, I served in a leadership position.

When Reed talked about his years in the College Republicans, I remembered heading up the campus ministry program, where I adopted a grandfather, served as a Big Brother, helped in planning campus church services, and organized the canned food drive.

His dream was to run for office or run campaigns, mine to be a minister. While he studied political science and history, I went off to divinity school. About that same time, he had a born-again experience, and I came out as a gay man.

A turning point for Reed was at a town hall meeting in Virginia, when he was almost knocked off his cherished local political committee by religious conservatives and had the realization that there could be a great political opportunity there. While I was working at Harvard's chapel, having been ordained, I realized there wasn't too much of a future in the traditional sense for an openly gay minister, and followed my calling by fighting for justice on behalf of the gay community.

In 1990, I had the honor to work in support of William Weld's first gubernatorial campaign and I had a vision of a new strategy for gay politics, while Reed remembers his first meeting at that time with Pat Robertson. I was struck by the fact that Reed, like most politicos, started with a dream of political power and found the cause that might carry him, while I was raised with religious principles and found the political arena as the place where our culture debates justice. The ultimate irony in this is that today, as a gay leader, I am denounced most by those who do so in the name of God, and Ralph Reed, although no longer at the Christian Coalition, still claims to speak for people who are pro-family and pro-faith.

As you might expect, the gay movement hasn't welcomed me with open arms either. But by being the outsider of the gay movement, I'm more open to insights and new

ideas missed by the knee-jerk, politically correct establishment that dominates gay thinking. In the same way that it is
often the expatriate writer who sees things at home from a
new and more interesting perspective, I hope that having
been a free thinker in a movement with little patience for
diversity, I may be able to offer some new insights, which
I've set forth in this book.

What I know of my family history gives me some personal historical background for being a political outsider. If
my sexual orientation is or isn't in my genes, my willingness
to stand against the current political labels and conventional wisdom seems to be. My best-known relative was Dietrich Bonhoeffer, a German Lutheran minister who
challenged Adolf Hitler and the rise of Nazism in his country. He taught at the Union Theological Seminary in New
York in the 1930s, but returned to Germany to combat the
scapegoating of Jews and other minorities in the name of
national unity. Upon his return to Germany, Bonhoeffer
joined the leadership of the anti-Hitler resistance while
serving in the military. He was arrested for preaching
against the government and for helping Jews escape. While
in prison, his role in the plot to assassinate Hitler was un-
covered. A few days before the Allies liberated his prison in
1945, he was executed.

In a biography of Bonhoeffer, *A Life in Pictures*, it is
noted that his grandfather's marriage to Julie Tafel
"brought a revolutionary element into the Bonhoeffers' an-
cestry. Here we find members of student fraternities, passionate republicans and socialists, Swedenborgians and

emigrants. Julie's father Frederick Tafel and his brother Gottlob were for a while expelled from Württemberg as student activists and democrats."

With the exception of the socialists, that all seems to make sense as part of my background. And while many find my political affiliation an oxymoron, others are more confused by my religious background. Far from seeing it as a barrier to my work on behalf of justice for gays and lesbians, I am fundamentally inspired by my Christian faith to combat injustice when I encounter it. Being disliked in one's political party or within one's community is a position few could or would withstand, but I'm able to do my work because of my understanding at a deeply personal level of the love of God. The prophetic voice of Christianity inspires all of my work.

In 1990, I got my political education. I managed the campaign of a Massachusetts state representative candidate named Mike Duffy whom I had met while he was at the Kennedy School of Government and I attended the Harvard Divinity School. We were introduced because, our friends assumed, we were the only two gay Republicans at Harvard. But Mike's campaign brought us into contact with the much larger gubernatorial race in Massachusetts that year, where I got my first introduction to gay politicos.

Before that I purposely stayed away from a gay political scene that largely focused on issues that seemed too liberal to me. I occasionally attended a fund-raiser and had volunteered as an AIDS buddy, but that was about it. That year, I watched as William Weld, the Republican candidate for governor, went from being someone with little understanding or interest in gay rights to becoming a crusader on the issue.

I watched a gay leadership, gripped by partisan Democrat identity politics, try to find an excuse to support the Democratic nominee for governor, John Silber, who, while president of Boston University, had once compared homosexuality to bestiality. I watched as the two openly gay Democratic members of the U.S. Congress, who had piously harangued anti-gay conservatives, calling them hypocrites and hate mongers, faithfully endorsed the homophobic Silber. Then, on election day, I saw a tide of gay and lesbian voters swing hard against the entire gay political establishment and vote to put a Republican in the State House. The whole experience forced me to rethink my politics and get some understanding of what we as gay people want and how we plan on getting it. I wondered how many other Republican candidates were being written off by gay political leaders who had developed close ties to the Democratic Party. I also realized that average gay voters were very different from the gay leadership that had come to represent them.

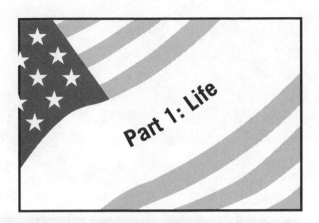

Part 1: Life

Oₙₗy ᴀ ꜰᴇᴡ ᴡᴇᴇᴋꜱ before the 1996 presidential election, a leading gay magazine, *Out,* sponsored a panel discussion at the National Press Club in Washington entitled "Out in D.C.—The State of the Gay Vote." The panelists were six "gay and lesbian leaders" chosen by the magazine. All of the dominant political perspectives and strategies in the gay and lesbian movement were represented.

To the far left sat Elizabeth Birch, executive director of the Human Rights Campaign, the gay community's largest and wealthiest organization. Next to Elizabeth sat Bob Hattoy, the outspoken Department of Interior appointee who had made national news when he spoke as an openly gay, HIV-positive man four years earlier at the 1992 Democratic National Convention. Next to him sat Keith Boykin, the executive director of the National Black Gay and Lesbian Leadership Forum and a former Clinton appointee. Boykin had just completed his book, *One More River to Cross*, about bridging the gaps within the black community over homosexuality. The moderator was *New York* magazine editor Kurt Andersen.

Next to him sat Carmen Vasquez, the executive director of the Lesbian and Gay Community Services Center of New York City. Next was Andrew Sullivan, the former editor of *The New Republic*, whose recent book, *Virtually Normal*, was still a best-seller in gay bookstores. On the far right I sat, the executive director of the Log Cabin Republicans, a gay and lesbian Republican organization. Just to round out the proceedings, the late Steve Michael, perhaps the most visible leader of ACT UP, sat in the audience with his cohort Wayne Turner, ready to join the discussion when he saw fit.

Earlier that morning, the press reported that the reelection campaign of President Bill Clinton was running ads on Christian radio stations around the country spotlighting the Clinton-Gore ticket's record on family values. After months in which Clinton had had a double-digit lead over Republican opponent Bob Dole, his ads boasted of his signature on the recently enacted Defense of Marriage Act, the most anti-gay measure ever passed by Congress.

The panel discussion became a debate almost immediately when the moderator posed the first question to Elizabeth Birch, wondering if in light of the radio ads, she felt that the Democratic Party was taking her for granted. The Human Rights Campaign had endorsed Clinton before even the New Hampshire primaries, and now as he steamed toward a landslide, he was using gay bashing in a clear attempt to gain even more votes. While pointedly not answering the question, Elizabeth returned to a standard line of her organization—any gay person who did not support President Clinton had to be "brain dead."

The moderator, not missing a beat, turned to me and observed, "I'm looking at Rich Tafel, and he doesn't appear to be brain dead."

I replied with an oft-repeated line of my own, that the gay movement's one-party political strategy of simply working within the Democratic Party had clearly failed. We were taken for granted by Democrats and written off by Republicans. My point was resonating within many parts of the gay community. There was a growing feeling that gays were being used for fund-raising, but getting very little in return.

Following my comments, Carmen Vasquez, a committed liberal, said: "Here's a first—I agree with Rich Tafel." She went on to explain how gays and lesbians at the grass roots were adrift, uninspired and discouraged by the many betrayals of the Democrats. Carmen predicted that she and many others would vote for a third party or "write in my lover's name."

Elizabeth, Bob, and Keith, while admitting that Clinton wasn't everything they'd hoped for, cautioned that every gay and lesbian person had a duty to go out and vote, and that Clinton was "the only choice," as the alternative was much worse. Instead of talking about the president's good points, they stressed the dangers of a Dole presidency. Elizabeth, in fact, repeated an HRC slogan in her call for high gay voter turnout: "We're simply voting for our lives when it comes to AIDS," she said, and she called for a defeat of the Republican Congress, calling it the "toxic 104th."

Steve Michael of ACT UP couldn't contain himself, and found his moment to join in. Standing up in the audience, he named all of Clinton's promises on AIDS from 1992, and went point for point to demonstrate how none of them had been kept. I also challenged Elizabeth about the Republican Congress's record on AIDS, pointing out that, while her rhetoric is very appealing to the average gay voter, the fact was that the Republican Congress had actually increased AIDS drug funding $100 million over Clinton's own spending requests only weeks earlier, and Bob Dole's record on AIDS was more distinguished than Clinton's when he first ran for president in 1992.

The debate about Clinton's record versus his rhetoric on gay issues continued, but the panel discussion turned next to which agenda gays were fighting for in the first place. Andrew Sullivan, who had written an anthology on gay marriage, lit into Elizabeth and her organization for "not lifting a finger" on behalf of the gay marriage cause. Elizabeth strongly denied the charge, shooting back at Andrew that "it is easy to give speeches and write articles" on behalf of issues, but "political work is much more complicated."

Keith Boykin dismissed the issue entirely, saying that marriage was not the most important issue within "gay communities of color," implying that Sullivan's comments reflected his racial and class privilege. Bob Hattoy joined in as well, cracking a deflecting joke: "If you want to go get married, do it! Just don't expect Bill Clinton to show up at your wedding."

And so it went for ninety minutes. If you read the literature of the far right in America, you'd believe that the gay community is a united monolith moving ahead full steam with a clear agenda. But even a cursory glance at reality would show otherwise. As this panel—and any representative panel of gay leaders—demonstrates with stark clarity, the gay movement is far from united on goals, agendas, strategies, and worldviews. And every such debate seems to raise more questions than it answers.

The election results that followed two weeks after our panel discussion offered few insights and more questions. One month before the election, Elizabeth's Human Rights Campaign had released a poll that ran on the front page of the *Washington Blade* showing that 88 percent of gays would vote for Clinton and 5 percent for Dole.

On election day, however, the *Blade*'s exit polls found that gay voter support for Clinton had dropped to 68 percent—a full twenty points in one month. Dole's numbers, on the other hand, were a surprise to anyone who thought of the gay community as universally liberal and Democratic. Dole captured 25 percent of the gay vote, five times greater than expected, and he received a higher percentage of votes from gays than from any other minority group in America. The *Blade* also found that gay voter turnout was at its lowest since tracking began.

Interviews with gay voters made it clear that in the gay community deep cynicism had replaced the widespread euphoria of just four years earlier with Clinton's emotional 1992 outreach to gays. It was a cynicism edged with bitterness, as Carmen Vasquez had articulated, but it clearly had led to apathy. In addition to disappointment with the president, gay voters spoke about a feeling of a rudderless gay movement. They felt there was no clear agenda and no clear direction and, thus, no strategy.

Like many gay people, I found myself asking a multitude of questions: Why does our movement feel rudderless? Why these incredibly different perspectives within our community? Which political strategy will best serve gays and lesbians? And yet, with such divergent experiences, there is still, in my view, a single answer to the overriding question—what do gays really want and what strategy will take us there?

The simple answer is that gay Americans want what any American wants—the right to life, liberty, and the pursuit of happiness, each realized in that order and each informing the next. In fact, the evolution of the gay movement from its beginnings in 1950 to the present echoes this sequence of struggles, beginning with the struggle for life itself—the struggle that arises from simply being different and facing the rejection of society. The next logical battle to be undertaken is the battle for liberty; this takes place in the arena of political debate, where the various responses to rejection can become ideologies. But the ultimate struggle of all gays and lesbians is the pursuit of happiness—the pursuit of the right to be happy with oneself and to live in a just society—and it is in this struggle that our values matter most.

Why a Gay Movement Now?

Gays and lesbians have come far since the 1950s, when *Newsweek* made a hard-news analogy between "queer people" and sex murderers. During the worst years of the Cold War, gays were considered security risks in the military and other branches of government, and the first ever government subcommittee—with the open-minded name "Employment of Homosexuals and Other Sex Perverts Committee"—had been established to investigate gays in the federal workplace. Both political parties, as well as the ACLU and the left-wing counterculture establishment, from the Communists to the beatniks, were anti-gay. This seemed hardly a good time to start a movement for gay equality, so what events allowed for the first American gay rights movement in 1950?

Worldwide trends that may seem remotely connected to the creation of a successful and sustained gay rights movement were sweeping the world at that time. Futurist Alvin Toffler's 1980 best-selling book *The Third Wave* describes the winding down of a second major worldwide age around 1950 and the beginning of a "Third Wave." This Third Wave followed the agrarian age, the First Wave, that dominated society for almost ten thousand years, and the relatively brief Second Wave, what we know as the industrial age. The Third

Wave is the information age. Each wave of economic revolution brought with it tremendous social, legal, cultural, and political change.

During the shift from the agrarian age to the industrial age, all major social institutions changed. The most dramatic change came in the family moving from an extended arrangement to a condensed nuclear family to meet the needs of industrial economies. The family of the agrarian age had been a large, extended, immobile economic unit rooted in the home, where the number of kids you had, particularly boys, determined the number of workers you would have for the family's main activity for earning income, such as tilling the fields. In addition to providing cheap labor, children also became your social security system—the more children, the more likely the parents would have a decent life in old age.

But in an industrial society, children weren't your labor anymore. Most often everyone in the family worked for someone else. For the first time in world history, childbearing gradually shifted from a necessity to a luxury. Institutions were created to meet the needs of the new family and mobility became a requirement. Although few gay people realize it, their own freedom was ordained in America's shift into this free market, industrial-capitalist society.

So, while gay people have been around since the dawn of time, only in the post-agrarian society could a culture tolerate nonprocreative members to any great extent. America's industrial age led to mobility and to urbanization, further laying the groundwork for the possibility of gays coming together as a community. With these worldwide trends, the stage was set for a gay culture to come out of the shadows. For centuries gays and lesbians had married, had kids, joined religious orders, or simply described themselves as "not the marrying kind." But that was about to change, and the information age would only speed up the pace of these dramatic shifts.

The gay community remains very diverse, despite the fact that over the past thirty years certain leaders of the gay establishment have tried to convince gay people that there is a "gay" way to act, dress, eat, converse, walk, socialize, shop, a gay place to live, and even a gay way to vote. Gays in fact share only two fundamental qualities—a sexual attraction to and love of people of the same sex, and an awareness of the societal rejection that results. Two items that often build bridges between gays or lesbians who meet are mutual attraction, and a mutual sharing of "coming out" stories. Gay people, for all their differences, share a common rejection by society and, very often, by family and friends.

While this rejection has been almost universal, responses to it have been quite different. Understanding these different responses is the best way to understand the political outlook and strategies each gay or lesbian person will use to achieve personal freedom.

Scholars who analyze the gay community have most often described it as made up of two warring camps: "assimilationists" or "mainstreamers" versus "liberationists," "radicals," "militants," or "progressives." While these categories are more helpful than the left-versus-right or liberal-versus-conservative labels, they still don't account for the true diversity of thinking in the gay and lesbian community. In observing the *Out* panel, there was much more going on there than liberal versus conservative or assimilationist versus liberationist. I'd argue that the gay rights movement has been pushed and pulled by three navigating belief systems since the very beginning: assimilationists, liberationists, and libertarians, with the libertarians having been left out by most scholars.

Assimilationists

By far the most popular, dominant, and therapeutic reaction to rejection is that of the assimilationist. The first, most common, and currently most popular response to rejection is: "Don't reject me, I'm just like you. I'd like to be liked."

On the *Out* panel, Elizabeth Birch and Bob Hattoy represent the assimilationist perspective, but the desire to be liked has always been at the core of large parts of the early gay movement. The assimilationists met a very basic human need of gay people who had experienced rejection—they made them begin to feel good about themselves. The therapeutic culture came into its own during this period of the early gay rights movement, and the assimilationists represented the marriage of these two in a therapeutic political movement often more concerned with offering its members a sense of pride than with effecting political change. The early meetings of the first gay organization, the Mattachine Society, resembled today's group therapy sessions more than any political meeting. Their goals were first to create a safe place for lesbians and gays to come out, and then to convince themselves and the straight society and each other that they were not degenerates. So desperate were they to be seen as being in the public mainstream that they were actually thrilled when an invited expert came to speak, even though these experts often condemned the homosexual lifestyle as deviant.

The Daughters of Bilitis, a lesbian alternative to Mattachine, was another assimilationist organization whose meetings were therapeutic. Members described their group as "a self-help effort for women, a haven where they could experience a sense of belonging, put their lives in order, and then, strengthened and regenerated, venture forth into society." A circular for new members called it "a home for the Lesbian. She can come here to find friendship, acceptance and support. She can help others understand themselves, and can go out into the world to help the public understand her better."

The Mattachine Society incorporated both assimilationists and liberationists. Founded by a liberationist named Harry Hay, it quickly purged him from the leadership, and went on to represent exclusively the assimilationist strategy for gay rights.

Of the three strategic responses, the assimilationists offer the least in underlying philosophical principles to support their outlook, goals, and strategies. They often describe their political strategy as simply pragmatic, and their outlook is much more a response to feelings—an example of a therapeutic approach to political change. Seeking ways to be more acceptable is a natural and common human response to rejection. The commonality of this striving in society generally helps explain the success of this strain of the gay movement, as assimilationists will find many empathetic straight people who understand rejection and pain.

★

The gay organization that best represents the assimilationist perspective is the Human Rights Campaign, which was known until 1994 as the Human Rights Campaign Fund. This organization does not have an "in your face" name. In fact, the name sounds just like that of any other human rights or civil rights group. The group's logo—an equal sign—represents the desire of most gay people just to be treated the same as everyone else, to downplay differences.

Some liberationists have called HRC "the Champagne Fund" and have kidded that the organization should replace the equal sign with a black bow tie, as black-tie dinners are a prime source of income for HRC. And though the organization may have its critics, no one can say that it doesn't know how to raise money. Today, HRC has an annual budget of more than $12 million.

The black-tie dinner is a metaphor for the assimilationist strategy. It makes attendees feel good about themselves, even elite. It minimizes actual political talk and offers attendees an evening that sends one message: We are good, we are elite, and we are powerful.

I attended my first black-tie dinner in Dallas. Almost every major city in the United States holds a dinner for

HRC. The Dallas dinner is the largest in the country; it is now the largest charity dinner in the country. Table captains and co-chairs plan it for an entire year.

The dinner I attended was striking on a number of levels. First, it was loaded with gay Republicans and Democrats, each boasting about how many tables he or she bought that year. I stood in the lobby and watched every type of luxury car and limo drop off guests. They were in black tie and some even had furs.

The program was decidedly unpolitical. A montage in the beginning featured Angela Davis, who screamed, "Gays and lesbians are crucial. They are the only thing left of the left." The audience gave very little applause. Then came Barry Goldwater, who talked about the importance of gays in the military; the room burst into applause and screams. The speakers included the Democratic governor of Oregon and a Democratic member of Congress, and the audience seemed appreciative that these straight people had told them they were good. But the guests were really at this event to see and be seen. They'd grown with the knowledge that Dallas, like most major American cities, held elite charity balls. They were simply imitating what they had seen growing up and creating their own sense of belonging.

I was most struck by my conversations with the Republican attendees. They couldn't stop boasting about the size of the Dallas event. They told me again and again how many tables they had sold. When I asked them about the speakers, they just gave me blank looks. When I told them that most of the political money raised went to Washington,

D.C., where it most likely went to liberal Democrats, they got defensive. Their attitude was "Please don't bring politics into this." This event was about empowerment and feeling good. They had been rejected for being gay, yet now were part of the biggest charitable dinner in Dallas.

The assimilationist portion of the gay community is very feelings oriented. They have a strong desire to overcome rejection and become accepted. Politics is a way for them to feel good about themselves. HRC taps into that deep need for acceptance and raises money off it.

Liberationists

Though assimilationist and liberationist are usually both considered liberal and both are active in Democratic politics, their responses to rejection are very different. While the assimilationist feels bad for being rejected, and seeks to be liked, the liberationist responds with rage: "If you don't like me, then fuck you!" Liberationists see their differences with society, while the assimilationists see only similarities.

Carmen Vasquez, Keith Boykin, and Steve Michael represented the liberationists at the *Out* panel. This helps explain their questioning of Bill Clinton and issues like gay marriage. The National Gay and Lesbian Task Force is the most highly visible organization today representing this point of view. Liberationists have been the most visible and vocal in responding to rejection. They have held only brief periods of dominance, but their impact has been much greater than their numbers. Nearly all of the gay historians have written from a liberationist perspective, attacking assimilationists and ignoring libertarians. While the assimilationists tend to base their strategy on hurt feelings and a need to be liked, the liberationists turn their hurt feelings into rage, expressed with a mix of New Left politics (drawn heavily from Marxism), socialism, and anarchist thinking.

One liberationist at an early Mattachine convention summed up the difference this way: "Today's gay liberationists still hold to a Marxist critique; they believe that injustice and oppression come not from simple prejudice or misinformation, but from relationships deeply embedded in the structure of American society."

In complete opposition to the assimilationists' effort to win over straight society, the liberationists saw gays as rebels against America's traditional institutions, which they found oppressive.

Liberationists can also lay claim to the founding father and original thinker of the gay rights movement—Harry Hay. He was a music teacher at the People's Education Center in Los Angeles. At the height of the Cold War, he was an acknowledged member of the Communist Party of the U.S.A. and a onetime hopeful observer of the Communist movement in Russia. Much of what is now considered "queer" political thought has its origins in the Marxist worldview of its earliest leaders. Hay, like Marx and Lenin, experienced police brutality, which has a lot to do with his outlook on authority. At the time, Hay was optimistic about the Soviet Union as a potential model country for treating homosexuals equally. Immediately following the Russian Revolution, criminal penalties for homosexuality were dropped. Of course, the Soviet Union's honeymoon with such attitudes didn't last very long. During the Stalin regime, homosexuality was recriminalized and punished severely.

But many American Communists still held hope that there would be more tolerance for gays through a "true" Marxist revolution. However, anyone who thought that Marxists/Communists were somehow predisposed to supporting gays was in for a surprise, as was Hay. He came out to party superiors, who told him to keep it quiet. He took their advice and in 1938 married another party member, isolating himself from gay social circles and publicly conforming to acceptable sexual standards. Later, however, Hay refused to repress himself to please fellow Communists. He divorced his wife and set out to build a network of fellow gay travelers—mostly fellow schoolteachers in Southern California.

While the Communist movement wouldn't tolerate Hay's sexual orientation, he had gained organizing experience from years in his secretive Communist cell network, which served him well in organizing a clandestine gay movement. When he created the Mattachine Society, he modeled it directly on the Communist cell structure, which kept its members anonymous, yet part of a growing network. This worked well in the early years, when membership in Mattachine could itself be grounds for firing from most any job. The concept of gays as a minority was a direct product of Hay's application of Marxist criteria.

As an avowed Communist in America in the 1950s, Hay was clearly on the fringe of American society. His outsider status allowed him a unique view of himself and society, free to imagine and offer visions of a gay culture. Hay envisioned gays as a separate people or tribe, a radical concept then and even today. He became frustrated when his organization grew and filled up with assimilationists who pushed out other liberationists like himself. Hay had a wild temper and his peers report again and again that he would storm out of meetings.

In the era of Senator Joseph McCarthy, new members in Mattachine were horrified to learn about their founder's Communist leanings. The fear of being labeled gay was bad enough, but to be tied to the Communist Party was terrifying. In Washington, McCarthy already had made the connection, and gays and Communists were being ferreted out of the government.

Hay's visionary, liberationist, and Communist ideals weren't tolerated long by the Mattachine rank-and-file. Though Hay was knocked out of the movement's leadership, his idea that gays were a distinct minority in need of global revolution has had a profound impact on the gay movement.

One basic, defining principle Hay introduced, though rejected by the assimilationists, was that homosexual rights were part of a multi-issue strategy. Liberationists, like Hay, always saw gay issues as one of a cluster of social justice issues that required comprehensive societal change. Hay and his fellow organizers were no shrinking violets when it came to choosing "related" gay issues that reflected this multi-pronged approach. In 1953, at the height of America's involvement in the Korean War, the Mattachine Society, in one of its first acts, circulated an anti-war petition. The society spoke of "an alliance between capitalism and land-holding elites" in the United States. It would make for a great trivia question today to ask: What was one of the key issues of the early gay rights movement? Few would guess it was opposition to the Korean War.

While Karl Marx is famous for his call to arms—"workers of the world unite!"—gay liberationists adapted it for themselves: "All oppressed minorities of the world unite!" Hay actually tried to build a gay history on the Marx-Engels paradigm of savagery, barbarism, capitalism, and socialism, claiming that a homosexual-accepting, matriarchal society somehow predated male-dominated savagery.

Hay believed gays had to join the effort to overthrow the capitalist system that was oppressing the poor, laborers, blacks, Latinos, women, Jews, and now gays and lesbians. They had to unite in a coalition to defeat those in power. They didn't want simply to be part of America and its institutions, they wanted to overthrow them. Many gays who were members of other minority groups were particularly drawn to the liberationist strategy.

In 1969, liberationist activist Carl Wittman wrote *A Gay Manifesto*, which summed up liberationist thinking. Spelling "Amerika" with a "k," as was popular among the New Left, his manifesto can be summed up by his line "Exclusive heterosexuality is fucked up."

He called for a coalition of women liberationists, black liberationists, Chicanos, white radicals and ideologues, hip people and homophile groups. His vision has become the core coalition of gay left politics to this day.

On June 28, 1969, the liberationists came upon a major breakthrough in their struggle with the assimilationists for dominance in the movement. On that evening, the infamous riots began at the Stonewall Inn in New York's Greenwich Village. Gays and lesbians who had grown tired of police harassment fought back during a police raid. Their response escalated into a full-blown riot with police trapped in the bar, and patrons setting fire to police cars outside and battling riot control police.

The bar was in violation of many health codes, accused of dipping used drinking glasses into a tub of water and using them again, for example. Hepatitis spread quickly through patrons of the bar. The Mafia, which controlled the bar, extorted patrons through exorbitant fees and expensive drinks, and there was no liquor license. Usually the corrupt police investigators were paid off by the Mob to forestall such raids. It isn't clear whether this particular raid was a result of police not being paid off or another in a cycle of police raids to make Mayor John Lindsay look good in the upcoming election.

What really happened at Stonewall is less important than the mythology liberationist writers were able to create for a political community on the verge of getting organized. They were successful in capitalizing both on the political moment of the riots and, more important, in convincing America that this was the beginning—the defining flash point—of the gay movement.

The Stonewall riot was a perfect rallying cry. First, the action was an aggressive and militant revolt, not an accommodation. It was dramatic, helping to capture the imagination of followers. It pitted corrupt police, the system's institutional authority figures, against an oppressed group. The incident, and the legend, were a perfect metaphor and wonderful theater of the liberationists' vision and their reaction to rejection.

The Stonewall legend remains alive within the gay and lesbian community, as most obviously demonstrated by the number of gay pride festivals celebrated in June each year. Today, gays uncomfortable with the militant marchers are reminded to "remember Stonewall," and are told that "if it weren't for drag queens at Stonewall, we wouldn't have gay rights today." Ask anyone today when the gay movement started, and most will respond, "At Stonewall."

The liberation strategy was particularly attractive to lesbians, who didn't see much of value for themselves as the end product of assimilationist strategy. Although most early lesbian groups, such as the Daughters of Bilitis, were assimilationist, that changed in time. What really changed lesbians' views of themselves wasn't the gay rights organizations—most lesbians reported feeling unwanted by these male-dominated groups. Instead, lesbians found their political liberation in feminist groups, and none was more popular and influential than the National Organization for Women. This defection occurred despite the fact that, early on, Betty Friedan referred to lesbian activists in NOW as "the lavender menace," and called gay men "shallow."

In fact, lesbians quickly gained so much success in the feminist movement that feminist scholars often posited lesbianism as an ideal. If men were socialized to seek power over women through the patriarchy, under their worldview, then true feminists who fought the patriarchy by day but slept with men at night were selling out both themselves and the movement. Lesbians, particularly lesbian separatists, were the true model of independent, anti-patriarchal "womyn," free to actualize their true selves without men. Lesbian feminists demanded access and leadership. The identity politics of the New Left, whose rhetoric had been incorporated into the Democratic Party of the 1970s, flourished throughout the liberationist wing of the gay movement. No longer could one say "gay" without also saying "lesbian," when, in fact, "gay" was previously an inclusive name for both men and women. Through identity politics, words and labels became very powerful symbols of a person's thinking.

Like white lesbians, many black gays and lesbians identified with the liberationists' revolution against the corrupt system they'd experienced. Yet, like the feminists, they were not instantly welcomed into liberationist black organizations, such as the Black Panthers. In fact, Eldridge Cleaver, a leader of the Panthers, denounced homosexuality as "an evil as great as being chairman of General Motors."

The rage and courage of liberationists often come from the strong feeling of rejection they experience. Black, feminist, transgendered, and effeminate gays have often experienced layers of rejection because they are different. These layers of discrimination often cause them to favor overturning the entire system, seeing little hope in getting fair treatment otherwise.

★

My introduction to the liberationist wing of the gay movement came in 1991 when I encountered a group called Queer Nation. I was asked, as the head of Log Cabin, to speak at the University of Massachusetts at Amherst, where the Young Republicans were sponsoring a Straight Pride Rally in protest over gay and lesbian pride activities going on at the campus.

The Young Republicans had previously marked the anniversary of the 1978 assassination of Harvey Milk by handing out Twinkies. This gesture carried a double meaning. The man who killed Milk used as part of his defense the fact that he ate too much junk food, supposedly destabilizing his mind. This became known as the "Twinkie defense." "Twinkie" is also a widely used slur for gays. In addition, some of the Young Republicans had in the past carried posters claiming "AIDS Is the Answer," and now they were holding a Straight Pride Rally.

This would be a first for me, to join forces with radical group Queer Nation in denouncing a Republican group. However, I felt I had an obligation to speak out against their activities on the Amherst campus. A proud Republican, I did not want our reputation dragged through the mud by YR kids like these. Jason, the Queer Nation organizer, also asked if I'd be willing to call up the Republican club leaders and petition to be one of their speakers. I agreed, but to no avail—the Republicans never returned my calls. My close friend and fellow Log Cabiner Abner Mason agreed to join me on my trip to the campus. I prepared him for the possibility that we might be subjecting ourselves to verbal and even physical assaults from members of this Republican club.

We were greeted at the rally by a young kid wearing a Fidel Castro hat, T-shirt, camouflage pants, and purple high-tops. I knew it had to be the Queer National, Jason, who welcomed us into the messy office. One very friendly young woman introduced herself as a member of the steering committee. "Thanks for coming, we really appreciate it," she said. Another student yelled across to me, "Are you from Queer Nation's Boston chapter?" I responded, "Just the opposite, I'm president of the Log Cabin, gay Republicans." He responded with a shocked look, but continued cutting out pink triangles for posters.

Jason again asked me to pursue his idea of having me attempt to speak at the Straight Pride Rally. "They won't let you speak, but it will make them look really bad when they don't." As we left with Jason to find the Republicans, I overheard a young man ask, "Does anyone know where the 'Rape Is a Man's Issue' buttons are?"

Jason presented me to the Young Republicans and took a few steps back to watch the confrontation. These guys in their suits and suspenders looked visibly nervous when I introduced myself as head of the gay Republicans. One of them surprised me by asking, "Log Cabin, right?" I questioned them about the charges, the Twinkies, the posters, and their hateful comments. They confessed that a lot of it was true; however, they insisted it came from only a few stupid loudmouths. "We are oppressed by the liberal agenda here," one commented. Another contended that the only way their group got any media coverage or support was to be militant, loud, and controversial. Where had I heard that before? Queer Nation's literature?

After some discussion about my recent support for the Gulf War and my fund-raising for Bush in 1988, I had them convinced as to the validity of my Republican credentials. Now I began working on the gay issue. First, I dispelled their misconception that the state's gay rights bill would eventually be a quota bill. Next, I spoke about the Republican philosophy of small government, small enough to stay out of everyone's bedroom. It was not long before they were coming around on the gay issues too. I realized that it was likely that no one had ever tried to talk positively to these guys about gay rights. Instead, they spoke of the oppressive PC culture that stifled their questions and opposition to the gay rights movement.

I'm not sure what the long-term impact of my conversation with those young radicals was. And I can understand why gay students who have been attacked so personally wouldn't want to engage these young conservatives. But I'm amazed at the impact of sitting down with people opposed to gay rights and building on the common ground we share, then moving to the issues on which we disagree. One thing is certain: These Young Republicans were much more likely to move in the direction of being gay-supportive and less viciously anti-gay when I answered their questions that day than when they were shouted at by those in Queer Nation or subjected to campus speech codes.

They decided they would put the question of my speaking to a vote. At the Young Republicans' office, one leader said, "Rich is a real conservative and he is the head of a gay Republican group, and I think he should speak at our rally." One member, Ted, who was typing away, stopped abruptly, and mouthed "What?" Ted, I soon realized, was the rabble-rouser of the group.

Ted rose from his seat and began a litany of questions starting with *"You're* a conservative?" After another Republican credentials check, Ted appeared impressed, but not convinced. Finally, he got to what was really driving him. He asked a religious question, to which my friend Abner smiled and said, "Rich went to divinity school."

"You went to divinity school? Let me guess. Harvard, right?" I nodded. "Didn't you find it a little . . . liberal?" he asked, smiling.

"Yes, parts of the school were ridiculously liberal," I responded.

"And you admit it?"

"Yes, I lived through it."

"Wow! How do you explain Romans and Sodom and Gomorrah?" he asked.

I responded with a biblical argument, but eventually gave a personal, theological argument using the language I had been raised on in the Baptist church. After more discussion, Ted grabbed his head and said, "Wow, you're really confusing me."

Then some more members of the club walked in. Ted introduced us, saying, "This is Rich and Abner, they're gay Republicans and they are going to speak at our rally today."

It was a done deal. We returned to the gay and lesbian student office to tell them the good news. Jason looked puzzled, almost disappointed with the news. "Don't trust them," he advised.

At noon we made our way to the front of the student

union for the rally. There were about twenty-five Republicans present, and a growing crowd of protesters, later estimated by police at six hundred. Using whistles, bullhorns, and chanting, the Queer Nation group was determined to shout down any speaker. Jason had informed me earlier that the Queer Nation organization had sent protesters to Amherst from as far away as New York and Boston. TV stations, as well as *The New York Times*, were covering the event.

Only police barricades kept the opposing groups separated. I immediately spotted a guy behind the Republicans walking with a huge sign that read, "Die Fags Die" and "Burn Fags Burn." I went up to the sign holder and demanded that he take it down. He refused; that was my first real resistance from the Republicans all day. After some shouting at each other, he waved his sign one last time for the cameras, and then disappeared.

I planned to direct my speech at the Republicans, who needed to be more sensitive to the gay community. I planned to attack that sign holder particularly. I also wanted to list the major steps that Massachusetts governor William Weld had taken on behalf of gays. But my hosts, Queer Nation, were screaming so loud that the president of the YR club was unable to introduce me.

When I began to speak, claiming to be both proud to be gay and proud to be Republican, the crowd quieted a bit. I waited for silence. While I was waiting, Abner pointed out to me that the kid who had carried the "Die Fags Die" poster was now standing in the crowd with the Queer Nation contingent screaming anti-Republican chants. That was quite an eye-opener even for my cynical eyes. I then spotted Jason, my host, in the front row with a sign that read, "Republican Assholes Just Need a Good Fuck!" He joined in the screaming so that I was unable to be heard. I felt betrayed. The same gay activists who had begged me to attend and begged me to speak were now screaming at me. I screamed over the protesting gay activists that the only way to overcome homophobia was through persuasion, not intimidation.

I decided to continue speaking, but to little avail. I spoke about being a gay Republican to shouts of "Sellout!" I spoke about Governor Weld's pledges and actions to end homophobia in Massachusetts to shouts of "Bullshit!" A few of them began chanting, "Fuck-ing Na-zi! Fuck-ing Na-zi!" Ted, the right-winger among the Republicans, stepped in front of me and yelled into the microphone, "Shut up, you losers, he's one of you." I ended my talk warning them that their decision to stop free speech would come back to haunt them.

When other YR speakers engaged in anything slightly homophobic, I would tell them to wind it up, and, to my surprise, they listened. Later, though, the campus police moved in to separate the two groups as Queer Nation began pushing down the barricades. I turned to Abner and said, "I warned you we might get physically attacked, but I didn't realize it would be the gays who would be attacking us."

Queer Nation members broke into a chant: "Homosexuality is natural, heterosexuality is not!" The young lesbian woman from the steering committee who had earlier thanked me for coming came through the crowd and apologized sincerely for the rude reception we had received.

"When Queer Nation is involved, you never know what will happen," she conceded.

As we left the event and headed for our car, one of the Young Republicans ran after us to invite us to lunch. We were appreciative, but declined. Only later did we learn that as we were leaving Queer Nation stormed the student union and ransacked the Young Republicans' office.

A year later at the gay pride event in Springfield, Massachusetts, a young man came up to me in motorcycle gear holding his helmet.

"Do you remember me, Rich?" he asked. I had no idea who he was. "I'm one of the Young Republicans from Amherst. I thought you were great. A few of us later came out, no thanks to those guys in Queer Nation."

Queer Nation would eventually disappear from the gay political movement, after being around for a couple of loud, obnoxious years. But the liberationist reaction in gay politics has been a part of the movement since its founding, and is alive and well. Today, the National Gay and Lesbian Task Force, ACT UP, and Sex Panic are all examples of liberationist gay organizations.

Libertarians

The libertarians in the gay and lesbian movement usually have been labeled assimilationist, although a few with anarchistic views have been called liberationist. But their response to rejection is very different from those of the other two groups. When confronted with rejection, the libertarian responds: "I don't really care what you think of me. I'll make new friends or I'll go work somewhere else. You just don't know me." The libertarian tends to see himself as a complex individual whose sexual orientation is but one facet of his life, and rarely the most important one. He believes he is personally responsible for his own successes and failures, and rejects the victimization claims of the other two groups.

Both Andrew Sullivan and I represented two different libertarian perspectives on the *Out* panel. Before my card-carrying friends in the Libertarian Party attack me for my loose use of the libertarian label, let me explain that I'm using the expression "libertarian" here in the sense of "classic liberal," meaning someone who generally believes in individual rights, individual responsibilities, restricted government, and free market economies.

Histories of the gay movement divide it into two categories—liberationists and assimilationists—with no mention of the libertarians. Party affiliation is a quick way to see how these three categories play out politically. The gay Democrats are, for the most part, divided among liberationist and assimilationist. The other third of the gay community, those who vote Republican, are overwhelmingly libertarians. But it is important to note that not all gay Republicans are libertarians—many are assimilationists. And not all gays who are libertarian are Republican—there are gay Democrats who prefer the libertarian ideals of individual rights and the importance of free markets.

The libertarian wing of the gay movement has heretofore remained invisible, much like gay Republicans. The impression that all gays are Democrats is shattered during each election when exit polls show that one fourth to one third of gays vote Republican. And many of those who vote Democratic do so more comfortably now that the Democratic Party has moved away from big government and spoken out in support of individual rights.

I once had a fight with a representative of Overlooked Opinions, a gay polling company, which claimed that less than 10 percent of the gay community was Republican. I asked the company representative where he gathered his data.

"At gay pride parades, gay bars, and through surveys done from gay magazine lists," he replied.

"But many gay people I know would never be found at any of those venues," I argued.

"Well, then they're not gay," he responded.

I was flabbergasted, but that discussion is just one example of the invisibility of the libertarians in the gay establishment consciousness.

One charge I hear continually when I speak before gay audiences is that gay libertarians are able to come out now thanks to the great pioneering work of liberationists and assimilationists. The implication is that the concept of a gay Republican is a new one and is a product of the courage of more radical activists' work.

But gay libertarians have been part of the gay movement from its very founding. Dorr Legg, one of the earliest gay activists and a leading libertarian thinker, made gay history when he won a Supreme Court decision in 1958 to permit *One* magazine, the earliest gay magazine, to be sent through the mail. A gay Republican who would later help found Log Cabin Los Angeles, he wrote an editorial for *One* that set forth the gay libertarian perspective, entitled "I Am Glad I Am a Homosexual." In his piece he attacked the assimilationists, saying, "They strive to desperately contort themselves into simulacra of heterosexuality."

He makes one of the earliest moral arguments that closeted behavior is immoral and ultimately unhealthy for everyone involved, and that gays should be proud and seek nothing more than equal treatment and individual rights, saying gays "should enjoy the same legal and social privileges as others, no more, but also, no less."

Unlike the vast majority of gays, including many libertarians, who were in the closet in 1958, Legg said, "I am homosexual. I am proud of it.... If society does not wish to accept me, or to understand me, that is not my problem, for, to paraphrase Louis, the Sun King's, 'L'état, c'est moi,' 'I am Society.' "

He wrote of individualism, morality, and religion in a positive way and took on those who desired to pretend all gays are the same. Not perceiving himself as a victim, he pointed out that there are advantages to being gay, noting that he could channel his creative energy into other areas while heterosexuals channeled much of their energy into procreation.

Libertarians are often confused with assimilationists who claim there is no difference between gays and straights. Here Dorr Legg's comments are timeless: "This is the individualism of the queen, flaunting makeup and a bracelet or two in the face of an amused or embarrassed public, and of the intellectual saying, 'I am proud of being a homosexual,' then throwing this declaration into the very teeth of public opinion." Over and over, Legg stresses the individual gay person, not the community. Gay rights for Legg are about personal pride and respect for differences.

Libertarians in the Legg tradition are not afraid of making waves or standing against conventional wisdom, whether gay or straight. He adds, "Do these concepts seem shocking, or startling? If so, the reader should prepare himself to be shocked.... Their [gays'] day is on the march.... Society is going to have to accustom itself to many new pressures, new demands from the homosexual. A large and vigorous group of citizens, millions of them, are refusing to put up any longer with outworn shibboleths, contumely, and social degradation."

The kind of therapeutic politics, emphasizing a new gay conformity, that was taking hold among the liberationists and assimilationists was rejected by libertarians, as Legg states with patriotic imagery: "Rugged individualism has an almost anarchistic quality that is yet as American as the 'hot dog.' ... It is in the spirit of the old Colonial flag, emblazoned with a rattlesnake and the motto 'Don't tread on me.' If there is one phrase that best summarizes the libertarian gay view of things, it is 'Don't tread on me.'"

David Brudnoy is one of the most articulate libertarians in the nation. I met David on his talk show in 1992, after returning from the Republican National Convention in Houston. After a caller harassed me about AIDS being God's punishment, Brudnoy spent the break offering some pointers on how to respond to that claim in the future. I knew that David was gay, but not that he was HIV-positive.

Two years later David would come out as a gay man with AIDS.

Since his coming out, he's written a book, *Life Is Not a Rehearsal,* which offers one of the best windows into the world of a libertarian gay person. He aptly describes the political philosophy of gay libertarians:

> It is a political philosophy that adheres to Jefferson on government—that government which governs least, governs best—but doesn't collapse into the swamps of anarchism. It is a political philosophy that admires the humanitarian Lincoln but not the Lincoln who tossed the Constitution aside when he felt that he ought to possess extraordinary powers. It is a philosophy that doesn't doubt Franklin Roosevelt's good intentions but considers his New Deal creation of huge government a platform for ruination, which Lyndon Johnson's Great Society marched merrily upon, since which the country has been going to hell in the proverbial handbasket.

Gay libertarians stress their individualism, so they don't accept the labels of identity politics. Instead they favor building one-on-one relationships with straight America without denying real personal differences. They're wary of big government solutions of any kind. They are individuals who believe it is important for each of us to take responsibility for his or her own life. Brudnoy sums up the libertarian attitude toward individual responsibility and against victimization:

We diminish our individuality when we console ourselves for our miseries by blaming others; it is unac-
ceptable behavior for men and women who struggle to
make their own lives meaningful and productive. The
victim game—"all my woes are the fault of somebody
else, anybody except me"—sets my teeth on edge.

Libertarians have a strong sense of public and private.
This sense, however, has too often led to rationalizing the
closet. I'm often told by gay libertarians that they don't
need to tell anyone they are gay because it is no one's business. But when I ask, "What do you tell colleagues or family
members about what you did on the weekend?" they admit
that they either avoid the topic or make something up.
They practice their own form of "don't ask, don't tell." This
ability to rationalize the closet is another reason libertarian
gays often remain invisible to observers of the gay community.

To be a gay libertarian, as Brudnoy learned, is to accept the wrath of both the gay left and the religious right,
although he found the attack from the left to be particularly startling:

When gay newspapers and commentators on radio
chastised me for not having come out soon enough,
for not becoming a one-issue spokesman, for not having insisted that everybody know of my HIV diagnosis
immediately after I knew of it myself, or for God knows
what, I began to understand how fractured, even frag-
ile, the gay community (so called) really is.

Being honest and standing in the middle can be rewarding, but being liked had better not be a priority. Brudnoy describes the contrarian nature of libertarian gays, and how he doesn't need the adulation of the crowd:

> I am a thrill seeker, pushing the limits of the acceptable, pushing at the envelope of what will pass muster, and expressing the bolder side of my nature by speaking truth on radio, never trying to please the thought police of political correctness, and becoming the same man in private and public.

Assimilationists, liberationists, and libertarians all hold different views of the promise of America. Libertarian gays, with their belief in individual rights, individual responsibilities, less government, and free markets, may be a uniquely American phenomenon.

Liberationists want to overturn the American system's oppressive structures, yet the same government that they don't trust in the area of civil liberties they trust to manage their health care and the economy. Assimilationists believe the government holds the solution to their problems, and seek to increase its power and involvement in the private sector to protect them from anti-gay forces. Libertarians believe firmly in the promise of America's Constitution to uphold individual rights, and they question any increased role of government in their lives.

Outside appearances can be deceiving. Libertarians tend to be very forward-looking, free thinkers, contrarians, and more often libertine than puritanical; they are more than willing to stand up against the status quo with a view of what should be.

The libertarians' response, while couched in the language that their gayness isn't a big deal, is most often wrapped in fear. This group, more than the other two, generally can pass for straight, and chooses to. Unlike many in the assimilationist and liberationist wings who can't pass for straight, the libertarians often must actively decide to make their sexual orientation known. In most cases, libertarians have developed their political orientation long before they can make sense of their attraction to the same sex.

The Differences We Have in Common

In speeches I give to the Junior Statesmen, a group of very exceptional high school students from around the country who demonstrate leadership abilities, I offer the libertarian perspective on differences and individuality. I explain to them that being gay in America is really about being complex individuals with a variety of differences, and I avoid the identity politics they've heard about in the past. We all know what it is like to be different in some way or another. In fact, we should pity the person who has always been part of the in group, although I don't think there are many of them.

Each year, I ask the students to accept a responsibility. I explain that much is given to them as leaders and much is expected of them. I ask them to return to their high schools and seek out the kid who is different, the boy who is a sissy or the girl who's not pretty enough to be popular, the guy kids make fun of because he's overweight or a nerd. I tell them to take a moment to imagine that kid who is different, and make a real effort to reach out to him or her. The reality, of course, is that we all have experienced being different, and tapping into that feeling can make straights more sensitive to gays.

I share with them that I know what it's like to be that kid who is different, so much so that I even thought that I might be better off dead than so different when I was young. I was fortunate enough to know in my darkest moments that regardless of what other people felt about me, God still loved me. But not everyone knows that, so I plead with them to reach out to the kid who is different.

I end my speech by saying: "If you're Jewish in a Christian school, don't be afraid to be different. If you're black in a majority-white school, be proud of your difference. If you're an evangelical Christian, but your friends look down on it, don't be afraid of what you believe just because you're different. If there's a boy in your school who gets called a sissy or fag, don't be afraid to befriend him, because, believe me, I know, he needs a friend. If all of your friends are Democrats, but you think you might be a Republican, don't be afraid to be different. It is the people who are different that make the advances, that create the new ideas, who dream dreams and have visions of what can be, not satisfied with what is. So be courageous, and don't be afraid to be all that you are, even when sometimes you feel different."

Invariably, a connection takes place between those

students and myself. The air becomes charged, and some of the kids actually start to cry. Why do these comments have that impact? Maybe some are actually thinking about kids that they know. But if the many letters I receive following this speech are accurate, then these kids themselves feel different. In fact, all of us do in some way, shape, or form. I've touched the differences they feel, the differences that we have in common. Unlike the assimilationist who wants to downplay real differences or the liberationist who is intolerant of those who seem not to be "different" like him, the future gay movement must articulate that, yes, we are different, and that differences make us human.

These three very different reactions to rejection within the gay community have also led gays into very different political strategies.

Part 2: Liberty

"I Feel Your Pain"—The Identity Politics of the Democratic Party

"I have a vision of America, and you're a part of it." That was Governor Bill Clinton's statement on the evening of May 18, 1992, when he spoke at a fund-raiser for his presidential campaign at the Palace Theater in Los Angeles.

Standing in front of a glittery replica of the "Hollywood" sign, Clinton delivered an emotional speech to a crowded room of gay and lesbian Democratic activists. Those in the room burst into tears, and so did their candidate. He continued, saying: "If I could wave my arm and make HIV-positive go away . . . I would, so help me God I would, and I'd give up my race for the White House, for that."

With these statements, Clinton had captured everything that gay men and women had longed to hear from a presidential candidate—the personal became political. He didn't stop there. He gave his word he would lift the ban on gays in the military, sign federal legislation to end employment and housing discrimination against gays and lesbians, and lead a Manhattan Project–style effort to find the cure for AIDS under the leadership of an AIDS czar.

The event was organized by Los Angeles gay power broker and longtime presidential friend David Mixner, who would himself end up raising at least a quarter of the $4 million raised by the gay community for Clinton. The gala event cemented a thirty-year effort for gays to be an accepted part of the Democratic Party.

How, you might ask, did being gay become synonymous with being a Democrat? The journey from rejected political fringe to becoming political players in the Democratic Party was not an easy one. Gays weren't always in the back pocket of the Democrats. In New York, for example, the new Republican mayor, John Lindsay, was welcomed in 1965 by many in the New York Mattachine, who hoped his reform-minded administration would be better than the Tammany Hall–style corruption that preceded it. At that same time, the earliest anti-gay effort surfaced in Congress, where Texas Democrat John Dowdy introduced a bill to revoke the Mattachine's permit to raise funds. During his committee hearing, Dowdy referred to homosexuality as "revolting to normal society."

The early half of the twentieth century was marked by dramatic increases in immigration. The new immigrants usually began their new lives in America in urban centers. As their numbers grew within these cities, so did their political power. Gays, though already in America, also experienced an immigration of their own, most often from more rural areas to American cities. Cities, with their variety of people, had developed more tolerance for differences than had homogeneous rural areas. In addition, cities became some of the first places in America where being single wasn't suspect. And as cities grew, a sense of anonymity and, therefore, privacy also grew. Many gay historians credit the stationing of single men and women in cities during World War II with offering many gay and lesbian pioneers their first taste of urban life, and they remained in these cities after the war ended. Cities like San Francisco and New York were gaining a reputation in the 1950s for attracting the avant-garde and nonconformists.

By the 1960s, so-called Democratic machines were well-established political organizations within many major cities. At this time, Republicans were creating the suburbs; Democrats, meanwhile, had developed a Tammany Hall–style politics in which those who delivered votes received jobs in return.

The gays who moved into these Democratic enclaves often used the organizations of the immigrants who came before them. Gays began building their own neighborhoods, often gentrifying previously dangerous neighborhoods. They created their own political groups, newspapers, bars, hangouts, and festivals.

The key to political success for the established groups that made up the urban Democratic Party was the ability of each community to organize itself into a successful voting bloc. Gays quickly realized that their success as a movement would be wherever they could deliver votes to the Democratic Party. Gay leaders immediately knew that their own political success would lie in their ability to deliver their votes. Though gays came from Republican and Democratic homes, the Republicans were encouraged to leave their affiliation behind when they arrived in America's cities and become a part of the largest possible voting bloc on behalf of the movement's progress. Furthermore, to remain a gay Republican held little practical purpose in many cities because those cities voted their mayors and city councillors into office in Democratic primaries.

Despite the fact that Democratic Party machines consisted largely of white ethnics, union members, blacks, and Catholics, groups that were not natural allies to the developing gay community, gays organized their vote and as a result had to be reckoned with. By the 1970s and 1980s, the gay community had become a key player in the Democratic Party establishment. For Democratic city political bosses, a mere nod of acknowledgment would be sufficient to yield eager gay cash and votes.

The more radical gays who sought social liberation often found themselves in the far-left wing of the Democratic Party. They were still suspicious of the party leadership, and saw themselves as agitators rather than team players. As the politics of victimization and identity politics developed within the Democratic Party, though, the Democrats began to co-opt the rhetoric of the New Left, if not its revolution. Suddenly the liberationists were closer to the mainstream spirit of the party. But acceptance of gays and lesbians even within the radical New Left was not automatic. Blacks, feminists, hippies, unionists, and Communists all initially rejected gays and lesbians who wished to join the New Left coalition of the Democratic Party.

Gay men and women with a desire to participate in the political process were confined to following the orders of the few gays with political clout. Self-appointed gay leaders in urban centers wielded a lot of power within the community; not only were gays told where to live and eat, but they were also instructed how to vote. An example of this was when the Alice Toklas Democratic Club of San Francisco went to the extreme of flying in the only elected openly gay official in the nation, State Representative Elaine Noble from Boston, Massachusetts, to endorse the machine-chosen candidate, Art Agnos, and denounce openly gay Harvey Milk in his 1976 bid for a California State Assembly seat.

In cities with large concentrations of gay residents in separate gay neighborhoods, a gay voting bloc emerged. The numbers could not be ignored. And for the first time gays had a voice in the party. But gay leaders lacked a strategy to take their hard work in the Democratic Party beyond the cities. Gays who held leadership in the Democratic Party were able to get presidential candidate George Mc-

Govern to personally support a gay rights plank in 1972, only to have him later step back from such support.

By the 1976 presidential election, the gay Democrats attempted to reach beyond their urban base of power again. Activists forced their way into the Carter campaign, with little result, as Carter actively courted the anti-gay Southern evangelicals. He campaigned as the first born-again Christian, and thus woke a sleeping giant. Southern evangelicals were highly suspicious of Republican president Gerald Ford, who supported the Equal Rights Amendment, and whose wife spoke out in favor of abortion rights. Carter, in thrall to the Christian right, told gay Democratic leaders that he opposed all forms of discrimination, but would refuse to support a gay rights bill in Congress.

Television evangelist Pat Robertson, son of a former U.S. Senator from Virginia, actively campaigned for Jimmy Carter. When Carter beat Ford, gay activists and religious activists were both destined to be disappointed, however. In one of Carter's first speeches to the federal workforce in Washington, he admonished those in the audience to get married if they weren't already. Rarely in American politics had a president so personally brought his conservative social and moral views into the political realm.

Gay Democrats contributed money, votes, and many hours of campaign labor, but they also accomplished something more powerful, if less tangible—they educated their political colleagues through personal contact. They showed that gays were not depraved sexual predators, but members of the community and very much a reflection of the rest of the Democratic Party. The greatest legacy of gays toiling in the Democratic Party was the beginning of the process of breaking down the stereotypes that had been persistent barriers to any advancement in society. At the national level, the high point for the gay Democrats came when the White House's public liaison officer, Midge Costanza, agreed to meet with them in 1977. Despite President Carter's refusal to be a party to the meeting, it remained an important step for the gay urban Democrats, who could now go back to their communities and reassure other gays that they were justified in following their leadership.

By the 1980s the gay Democrats had made sufficient inroads to merit a historic speaking position at the 1980 Democratic convention. Jim Foster, a San Francisco power broker, laid out before the convention a list of concerns preoccupying the gay community, while a pro–gay rights plank was added to the platform, helped in part by the sixty-seven gay delegates. But gay victories came at a price for the party. Southern Democrats felt more distant from a party that now boasted a high-profile role for feminists, blacks, and now gays. The forty-year-old Democratic Party political coalition that had control of the Congress was deteriorating.

At the same time, the Republican Party was losing its voice of social tolerance, replacing it with a harsh conservative tenor. A Republican protesting the hard turn of his own party, as well as the failure of Carter's leadership, Illinois congressman John Anderson made history as the first candidate for president in history who campaigned in favor of gay rights. Had gay leaders maintained some electoral independence they might have flocked to this pro-gay Republican pioneer. But it was too late. The gay political establishment by now was deeply enmeshed in the Democratic machine, regardless of Carter's ideology or the fortunes of their party at the polls.

★

Once Ronald Reagan came to power in the 1980s, gay leaders had no access to the White House. As a result of their dependence on the Democratic Party, they developed a confrontational strategy of victimization of themselves, on one hand, and demonization of the party in power, on the other. Reagan had won owing nothing to the gay movement but much to the blue-collar Reagan Democrats and religious right. Oblivious to their own role in this victory, gay strategists dug in with a clear message of anti-Republicanism. This tack made it easier both to raise money and to explain the lack of successful legislative movement. At the same time, attacking Republicans gained them new support and credibility in the Democratic Party. This approach made everyone happy by fulfilling the assimilationists' basic need to be liked and the liberationists' to take on the so-called wealthy Republicans. For years the lack of progress in the national gay movement could be blamed on the evil Republican administration, to the point that simply saying "Reagan-Bush" was enough to explain what was wrong in the world for gays.

In 1980, the assimilationists formed the Human Rights Campaign Fund. Their bipartisan label broadened their fund-raising and marketing potential within the community, but they really had little interest in and access to Republicans. The HRCF could, with a wink to the Democratic National Committee, give a paltry amount to moderate or liberal Republicans in very safe congressional seats, which they would then show to their Republican donors as evidence of bipartisanship. This practice was particularly painless while Democrats held a firm grip on Congress.

More troubling to the cause of gay political organizing and destructive to the cause of gay equality was that the HRCF ignored the need for grassroots political efforts and pretended that real change could take place only in Washington. The HRCF put the bulk of its efforts into creating a status-seeking organization for gays that paralleled those in the wider straight culture. Much of this came in the form of glittering black-tie fund-raisers designed to give politically active gays a sense of acceptance and influence.

Prominent Democratic members of Congress often appeared at these dinners to give assembled donors a speech that reminded them of their special place in the party without touching too deeply on any gay policy issues. Then the event would invariably move on to the awards ceremonies and other feel-good entertainment to remind the guests of their position as leaders. In the end, these efforts created the opposite of a serious political outlet for gays. Instead of community leaders, the HRCF made stars of dinner committee members. Instead of grappling with the political issues that divided gays, the HRCF hammered home its message—the Democratic Party likes you, the Republicans hate you—while never addressing the real nettlesome issues that confronted gay Americans.

Despite other voices in the gay community who claimed the HRCF stood for the "Human Rights Champagne Fund," the organization grew throughout the 1980s. Part of the problem lay in the simple facts of human nature. To object to the HRCF was to open oneself up to the painful charge that you were either indifferent to the battle for gay rights or really not a meaningful member of the gay elite. By the 1990s, the HRCF's strategy of glitz and giddy self-love had proved very successful. It was at the pinnacle of gay political power.

Throughout the Reagan years, America grew more conservative, and liberationists, with their socialist worldview, lost power in the gay community. The AIDS epidemic, however, gave the liberationist movement purpose and visibility. In much the same way they did with Stonewall, liberationists appealed to the bulk of gays to vent their rage at what was happening. Gay men were dying and pleasant words wouldn't suffice. Liberationists painted the picture of a group under siege by forces beyond its control: an uncaring, complacent government and a sexist, capitalist, patriarchal, straight majority that remained unmoved. "People are dying," they chanted, and dying from an unknown disease. "Capitalist drug companies," interested only in profits, didn't see a market in trying to find a cure. Wealthy gay men would not find a class barrier to protect them from the epidemic. Liberationists immediately took on renewed leadership in the movement.

In 1987, Larry Kramer founded the AIDS Coalition to Unleash Power—ACT UP—in an effort to harness gay anger to fight AIDS and societal apathy. ACT UP became the nerve center of liberationist action in the late 1980s. Liberationists had long called for socialized government and national health care, and the image of a silent government in the era of AIDS was a rallying point. Relentless in its determination, ACT UP made demands upon American society in reaction to the crisis, and forced many real reforms upon America's health care system.

Liberationist leaders laid the blame for the AIDS epidemic almost entirely on the Republican president, Ronald Reagan. Nowhere in this story of AIDS that they put forward could there be any discussion of the personal responsibility of gay men for their sexual behavior. Because gay sex itself was seen as a key component of liberation, those who called for changes in that behavior were labeled traitors to the sexual revolution.

Their silence on the subject of personal responsibility remains a hallmark of the liberationists today. In 1994, I was attacked by ACT UP Washington (D.C.) in its newsletter for saying that personal responsibility could stem the spread of AIDS. I had said in response to ACT UP leader Steve Michael that "we shouldn't be unrealistic about what we expect government to do. Our community has its own responsibility when it comes to AIDS . . . those at risk for AIDS—including gay men—should be held responsible for taking necessary steps to prevent the spread of HIV infection. They should not expect the government, under a Democrat or Republican administration, to be responsible for personal decisions that may lead to HIV infection."

This was a direct repudiation of the "blame Reagan-Bush" mentality held dearly by the activists. Michael responded predictably. "When it comes to responsibility," he wrote, "no one is more responsible for the state of AIDS in America than the Republican Party. Sounds like [Pat] Buchanan's speechwriter is now writing for Tafel and Log Cabin. . . . Blaming gay men for AIDS is like blaming Jews for the horrors of Nazi Germany."

It took years, but the catharsis of the liberationists' anger slowly gave way to constructive assimilationist community programs. The defiant slogans of the early years were softened and co-opted as social service replaced street theater in the AIDS movement. And though gay leaders succeeded in stealing the AIDS epidemic back from the liberationists—artfully praising ACT UP for its vanguard role while politely suggesting that ACT UP's flamboyant leaders were ill-equipped to conduct the community's most important business, minding the immense bureaucracy of AIDS—they could not free themselves from the dogged assumption that gay equaled Democrat. The rallying cry shifted from "People are dying!" to "Vote Democrat because we are voting for our lives."

★

In the 1988 presidential campaign, Governor Michael Dukakis of Massachusetts was asked by Tim McFeeley, the executive director of the Human Rights Campaign Fund, why he refused to support a gay rights bill. Dukakis slammed his fist on the table and yelled, "Because it is wrong!" During his term as governor, Dukakis had actually taken a child out of a gay couple's home and placed it in the care of a heterosexual couple, where the child was then sexually molested and abused. It wasn't until the courts overruled Dukakis that Massachusetts gays were able to be foster parents again.

The growing tension between the liberationists and assimilationists within the Democratic Party accelerated during the Dukakis campaign. Liberationists strongly opposed Dukakis. "Dukewatch" activists followed him around the nation protesting his anti-gay policies. Scott Lehigh, a writer for the *Boston Phoenix* newspaper, wrote that "through the incompetence and cowardice of the administration, the controversies exploded into a national news story in which the administration's capitulation to homophobia ended up aiding and abetting the gay baiting of the Jerry Falwells and Jesse Helmses of the world."

When a reporter asked a Dukakis strategist what impact the gay protests would have on the campaign, he smiled and replied, "They're not going to hurt us in Iowa." The years of exclusive identification of gays with minorities and minorities with the Democrats finally took their toll. Not only had Republicans written off gays, but Democrats knew now they could take them for granted. The early successes in the 1980 Democratic convention had soured by 1988. The gay movement still had not figured out how to translate its success in the Democratic Party at the city level to the national level.

Rather than address the fact that gays were being written off by Republicans and taken for granted by Democrats, assimilationists described the 1988 campaign as a choice between the lesser of two evils. Yes, the Democrat was bad on gay issues, but the Republican was worse—end of story. The gay activist strategy of working solely within the Democratic Party had left, and would continue to leave, gay voters with a perpetual choice between bad and worse.

★

By the dawn of the 1990s, liberationist rage and assimilationist seduction had created palpable tension in gay politics. Liberationists had become less interested in organizing and more involved in street theater. Pleased with the media success of ACT UP, they created a gay spin-off group, Queer Nation. They insisted that the new word for gay be "queer." "Queer" was meant to "take back" the straight world's most cruel anti-gay term and claim it as a sign of new gay power.

The *Advocate,* a gay magazine, declared 1992 "the Year of the Queer," and liberationists began predicting that "queer" would replace "gay" throughout the community within the next few years. Richard Goldstein of the *Village Voice* predicted that a new Third Wave of queer activism had hit America: "The first wave was about visibility, the second was about community, the third's about identity." He predicted a successful decade for the liberationists. New slogans reflected the new thinking: "Out of the Closets and Into the Street" and "We're Here, We're Queer, Get Used to It!"

A bold, courageous voice for liberationists, Queer Nation presented the face of gay rage so distorted with pain it was difficult to sustain. In 1992, I picked up a flyer in Boston produced "anonymously by queers" which illustrated the unbearable intensity of feeling that Queer Nation was trying to mobilize. It was a document of the rejection and frustration felt by many gays but expressed here only anonymously.

"When a lot of lesbians and gays wake up in the morning we feel angry and disgusted. . . . I hate Jesse Helms so much I'd rejoice if he dropped dead. If someone killed him I'd consider it his own fault. . . . I hate Ronald Reagan because he mass-murdered my people for eight years. . . . I hate the fucking Pope, and I hate John fucking Cardinal fucking O'Connor." And the list of hates went on and on— the military, the medical establishment, education professionals, *The New York Times,* even the art world—filling the rest of the page. On the back, the manifesto resorted to economical clarity. Over an illustration of a fist, it read: "I Hate Straights."

Despite its uncompromising message and visibility, or perhaps because of it, Queer Nation failed to strike a chord within the gay community. The fractious nature of the organization caused it to run amok, and within a year Queer Nation had devoured itself.

Queer Nation's failure created a vacuum that was filled by the assimilationist HRCF. In the Democratic Party primary of 1992, only one Democratic candidate for president lacked support from any significant part of the gay community—Bill Clinton. But once he became the nominee, the "bipartisan" HRCF had produced a flyer in support of him: "Tell the GOP in Washington: It is time for them to go!" Then, in bold print: "Support those who have supported us. VOTE AS IF YOUR LIFE DEPENDED ON IT."

Then the HRCF offered the solution and the promise. On the other side of the flyer, the heading read: "Why Gays and Lesbians Should Vote Democratic in 1992." Underneath were three promises: First, that Bill Clinton would sign a gay rights bill and end the ban on gays in the military. Second, that he'd lead "a real war against AIDS," including reforming health care. Third, that he would support the Freedom of Choice Act to guarantee reproductive choice for women. At the bottom of this political card was the expected union "bug" and a surprise in fine print:

> Endorsed by the Human Rights Campaign Fund, the nation's largest lesbian and gay political group. Paid for by the Human Rights Campaign Fund. Authorized by the Democratic National Committee.

The supposedly bipartisan HRCF had shed all pretense of interest in Republican candidates. The marriage between the HRCF and Democratic Party goals couldn't have been clearer. The Republican Party played its part too, by allowing its right wing to dominate its convention and make George Bush its pawn. A record number of gay Republicans would now vote Democrat in protest of the rightward leaning in their party.

★

The election of Bill Clinton and a Democratic Congress created a euphoria that swept through the gay community. Ironically, this victory would test the message of the gay

Democrats—that gays needed to work in only one party to obtain our agenda. The 103rd Congress and the election of Bill Clinton meant that the community could no longer blame Republicans for its lack of progress.

In addition, politics of victimization wouldn't carry the same weight, now that the "oppressors" had been politically vanquished. After finally winning the biggest contest of all and helping to take control of the American federal government, the HRCF's one-party strategy was about to fly apart under the first real pressure in its history. And it took a Democratic president and Congress to make it happen.

Within days of his inauguration, the glow of the celebrations still hanging in the air, President Clinton prepared to sign an executive order to lift the ban on gays in the military. Immediately, opposition sprung up from Georgia Democratic senator Sam Nunn, who led the opposition to Clinton's reform. Not only was Nunn against it philosophically, but he sought to represent the military establishment's disdain for Clinton's arrogant refusal to consult it, as well as the Senate Armed Services Committee's institutional pride—such a radical policy change would not be issued through the stroke of a pen.

A march on Washington by the gay community had long been planned for 1993. With Bill Clinton giving the appearance that he was backing away from his promise to lift the ban on gays in the military, it could have been the perfect opportunity for the president to reestablish his connection within the gay community. But Clinton hastily made plans to be out of town during the march, and the two wings of the gay political movement that had been united in their opposition to Republicans now began to debate among themselves.

Gay marches mean different things to liberationists and assimilationists. The liberationists wanted to prove how proud and radical they were by encouraging community members to make public every private fetish. As always, they hoped to send a message to straight society that the revolution was at hand. The assimilationist leaders, however, wanted to make the march a political statement that would demonstrate to the Democratic Party just how organized and powerful they were, and how valuable a part of the Democratic club they were and would continue to be. But more importantly, they wanted an event that left them feeling good about themselves.

To the frustration of liberationists, most gays came to the March on Washington in 1993 for the same reason they went to black-tie dinners. They wanted to feel that sense of connectedness, of belonging. Those who came to the march looking for the new leaders of their movement were the most disappointed.

The liberationists dominated the dais with shrill speeches about the evils of America and the panoply of discrimination against all the oppressed. Their messages were warmed-over 1960s rhetoric, uninspiring and annoying. Lesbian comedienne Lea DeLaria graced the viewers of C-SPAN with her observation that gay America "finally has a first lady we can fuck." The gap between the liberationists at the microphone and the community in general had only grown over time, cresting at this event. In the end, the

March on Washington was a celebration of feeling good rather than an effective political event.

The march didn't influence the president's decision on the military. Clinton turned his back on his promise to lift the ban, and that waffling reinforced the public perception that he had championed the issue to appease a liberal special interest group, and not because he believed in the issue in his heart. This may have been true. The gay leadership, stunned and humiliated, had to circle the wagons just to protect their own reputations. But the liberationists, who frankly didn't mind the assimilationist power brokers looking silly, happily and vocally charged Clinton with betrayal.

At a turning point during the military debate, David Mixner, the president's liaison to the gay community, waited for a call from Clinton aide Rahm Emanuel, with the hope that Emanuel would give him good news. Emanuel's response summarizes the feelings straight Democrats offer to their gay supporters who have nowhere else to go: "Who do you think you are? If the president of the United States never does another thing for you people, you should get on your knees and be thankful! He's already done more for you all than anyone."

Representative Barney Frank, an openly gay Democratic member of Congress and a Clinton loyalist, saw his Democratic president embarrassed on an issue where Frank could demonstrate his loyalty. He set forth to cut a deal on behalf of the gay community himself, by ignoring the gay organizations that were representing the community.

David Mixner described Frank in these terms: "Since

coming out of the closet he has been more determined than ever to have the approval of the Democratic liberal establishment. It seems clear to me that he decided that the way to be most effective was to be a powerful insider." The military compromise he engineered offered him that chance to prove his worth to his president and party; they could look good and the issue would go away.

When it was all finished, there was plenty of blame to go around. Frank blamed the gay leaders and Republicans, while gay leaders blamed Frank. Suddenly the old strategy of blaming the Republicans wasn't working within the gay community, which had just celebrated Democratic control of both houses of Congress and the White House.

The two most prominent Democratic gay leaders, David Mixner and Tim McFeeley, jettisoned their traditional assimilationist lobbying effort for the highly visible liberationist style—getting arrested in front of the White House in a sidewalk protest. These were the same people who had raised millions of dollars for the president in 1992, and who only months earlier had been delirious at the prospect of achieving a long-held dream. They had cried when Clinton told them that they were a part of his vision of America, and mailed thousands of copies of the tape of Clinton's remarks throughout the gay community. Now they were being arrested and handcuffed in front of the Clinton White House. Nothing better demonstrated how far the gay political movement needed to go before it would see real and substantial political power in America.

The debacle regarding the military was just one obvious embarrassment suffered by gay leaders. Under the next two years of Democratic control the gay community was beaten up like never before. The "don't ask, don't tell" compromise, which was supposed to allow gays to serve in the military as long as they remained closeted, in fact drummed gays out of the military in greater numbers than ever before. President Clinton now has the ignominious record of kicking more gays out of their jobs than any other president in American history.

Not only did a gay civil rights bill not get passed in that two-year period, but Democrats in the House, despite Frank's promises, never held a hearing. (Two years later when a Republican from Massachusetts, Congressman Peter Torkildsen, held a hearing, Frank condemned it in the *Boston Globe* as meaningless.) Senator Ted Kennedy did hold a hearing in his Senate committee in 1994, but the Clinton administration pulled its representative. (Only as the 1996 campaigning approached did Clinton agree to support a gay employment bill drafted to meet his requests.)

David Mixner sums up the sea change that took place once Clinton got elected: "After they took our money and our votes and secured their jobs within the administration, the hostile staff members decided the time had come to put us in our proper place." The frustration that followed came from the fact that the community was unprepared for this betrayal, and, having placed all its eggs in one basket, had little leverage.

During the president's first ever meeting with gay leaders at the White House, Mixner, who had put his reputation on the line to get gay support for Clinton, was not invited. Not one gay leader protested his being excluded. The personal betrayal Mixner experienced was only a taste of what was to come for the whole gay community. Examples abound: Early in Clinton's administration, Secret Service agents greeted gay visitors to the White House wearing rubber gloves. Clinton persistently refused to submit a brief in the Supreme Court challenge of the anti-gay Colorado Amendment 2. When the president signed an anti–gay marriage bill called the Defense of Marriage Act, he told gay leaders he "hated" signing the bill, and did it in the dead of night. Mixner sadly concludes his book, *Stranger Among Friends*, with the lesson of the Clinton administration: "We have been betrayed too often and we know it will happen again."

By October 1996, President Bill Clinton's reelection campaign had secured a solid double-digit lead over Republican Bob Dole. But simply beating Dole wasn't enough— Clinton wanted more. He began targeting the religious right, soliciting their vote by running campaign ads on Christian radio stations, saying that the liberal label for Bill Clinton simply wasn't accurate. The evidence of that fact cited in the ads was that Bill Clinton had supported and signed the anti-gay Defense of Marriage Act just weeks earlier. The ad boasted that Clinton was standing up for "our values."

Michael Kelly summed it up in the December 2, 1996, issue of *The New Republic* when he described Clinton as "a shocking liar" and "breathtakingly cynical. . . . A man who signed the Defense of Marriage Act while denouncing it as gay bashing, then ran campaign commercials on Christian radio bragging that he signed it."

Clinton had received millions of dollars over the past four years from gay Democrats. The Human Rights Campaign (as the HRCF was now known) endorsed him even before the New Hampshire primary. After four years of snubs and apologies, betrayals and makeups, blindsiding and condescending explanations to gay leaders who had done so much for him in 1992, Clinton cynically decided in his final campaign that he had nothing to lose and everything to gain by going anti-gay.

★

How could someone who had received so much from the assimilationist and liberationist wings of the gay movement thank them by running these anti-gay ads? Well, a look at his history and political behavior shows there was a clear pattern. As is evident in his charm, perhaps his greatest legacy, Clinton understands the longing to be liked and to belong better than any politician in American history. He is a product of the rise of pop psychology and the human potential movement, and perhaps as a result he has molded the Democratic base coalition of identity politics into the politics of therapy. It is no accident that he has emerged as the Great Empathizer.

During the four years of his first term, Clinton developed a personal style that won over all the various minority groups that had attached themselves to the Democratic Party, but he was most successful with gays because they were so emotionally needy. After each incident that angered the gay leaders, the president held a meeting. During the meeting, he would, like a good therapist, say, "I invited you here to listen." Attendees, their degrees of candor varying, would thank him, apologize to him, and vent their feelings. Like a good therapist, he would offer aerobic listening; he'd feel pain, maybe even tear up. And they loved it, leaving the meeting refreshed and revived. Observers, however, listening to the story of what went on inside, would scratch their heads wondering what of substance was accomplished inside the halls of power on that day.

One of the best eyewitness accounts of the effect of the therapeutic politics of the White House meetings is that of Lorri Jean, the executive director of the Los Angeles Gay and Lesbian Community Center. In her letter to donors describing her White House visit, she begins by telling the readers how special each of them is: "Because you're among my most generous friends, I want to write and share some wonderful news. I just returned from a trip back east which included a July 22, 1997, meeting with President Clinton! He wanted to meet with a small group of gay and lesbian leaders from around the country, and I am very proud to tell you that I was among those he invited."

Therapy sessions were not policy discussions: "We discussed the need to ensure that we not get bogged down in specific issue details," she writes. Everything was exciting, including the cab ride: "I loved telling the taxi driver, 'The White House please; northwest gate.'"

"That's me," she writes, gushing over the enclosed photo of her and Clinton at the meeting, "second from the bottom on the left—the one to whom the President is talking!" Even the place cards excited her: "hand-calligraphied place cards at each seat (complete with gold-embossed Presidential seal)."

She realized she was sitting across from the president and ate a cookie. She describes her reaction to the Great Empathizer, Bill Clinton: "His levels of dynamism and charisma are enormous, and he has a remarkable ability to look at you and make *you* feel like you're the world's most important person to him at that moment."

He must have been charismatic, because even the president's ability to change the subject from what the activists want to talk about to something he'd rather talk about is treated as a gift: "But most of all, throughout the meeting I was struck by the President's extraordinary ability to seem totally involved but never respond on point except when he so desired, and to talk and move the conversation entirely away from the topic raised—and [he] seemed to do it without people realizing what was happening until the end of his comments. What amazing skills!"

The whole affirmation session was succeeded by another. She says that afterward the participants all headed to the Willard Hotel for drinks hosted by a generous HRC donor.

"We joyously toasted each other for how well the meeting had gone," she writes. And she found herself wondering whether "people like Thurgood Marshall, or Martin Luther King, Jr., or Rosa Parks had shared similar moments of pride and glee."

Elizabeth Birch, executive director of the HRC, in her review of this second meeting between the president and gay activists, points out that she's met Clinton before. "I've never seen him quite like this. . . . He didn't want to leave. He stayed behind and wrote notes to people."

Brian Bond had just left his position as the Democratic National Committee's gay and lesbian liaison during the 1996 campaign and was heading up the Gay and Lesbian Victory Fund. He'd obviously seen the Great Therapist in action before: "He likes these events, and everybody feels good. My bigger concern is whether he is willing to expend the capital to make people in the White House responsive to our issues." I don't know that Brian will be invited to the White House, as the gratitude and praise of these group therapy sessions have very often come to be defined as the greatest achievements of the modern gay rights movement.

The HRC, which had egg on its face following the gay-bashing Clinton radio ads, explained those away by implying that they were not really part of the campaign, and had been created just by some guy acting on his own. This in spite of the fact that the ads kept coming. Creating and sustaining that type of blind devotion would require more than the oft-used White House meeting—much more. On almost the anniversary day of the debut of those ads, and close to the anniversary of the day he signed the Defense of Marriage Act, President Clinton attended an HRC dinner, where he posed before the group's logo so that cameras could capture the moment. All who attended told how they burst into tears when he spoke. The HRC would describe that dinner as its greatest accomplishment in the movement.

Liberationists lacked the enduring patience of their

assimilationist colleagues. They came to believe they had helped elect a moderate Republican in 1992, and he had undermined every part of their agenda. In a September 17, 1996, *Advocate* op-ed article, the bisexual leader of the National Organization for Women, Patricia Ireland, recalled being arrested in front of the White House in protest of Clinton's "don't ask, don't tell."

"Compared with the sharp sense of betrayal others felt that day, my emotions were muted—just as they were when I heard Clinton say he'd sign a bill banning lesbian and gay marriage. Perhaps that's because I never thought Clinton was the answer." She goes on to compare welfare reform to these other betrayals of gays, and then refers to the choice between Clinton and Dole as "Tweedle Dumb and Tweedle Dumber."

Liberationist Urvashi Vaid, in a bitter December 24, 1996, *Advocate* article, enumerated the Clinton betrayal of her faith:

> The *San Francisco Chronicle* ran a story headlined GAYS HOPING CLINTON WILL DO BETTER IN SECOND TERM. Based on what? His second term as the neoliberal, reinvented governor of Arkansas, the last time he won with the help of Dick Morris's come-stained fingers? ... All we have to use for leverage right now is hope—and the access of a few wealthy men. ... Wouldn't we rather believe we're safe? Would the Human Rights Campaign ever get invited to another dinner party at the White House if it said, "Hey, we did our loyal duty—he's in. Now let's pressure the squirmer from

Hope more than he has ever been pressured before—
call out the dogs"?

The National Gay and Lesbian Task Force's 1997
annual conference included a curious panel presentation—"Centrism and Its Discontents," described as follows:
"Democratic centrism is the guiding philosophy of the
Clinton administration, and the dominant ideology among
liberals today. What does centrism mean and what does it
mean to be gay, lesbian, bisexual, and transgender people?
Can work with the Democratic Party ever be a useful device
for progressive organizing?"

The growing cynicism within the liberationists couldn't
be clearer than in the laments of one of their great thinkers,
Michael Warner, in an *Advocate* piece in September 1997 entitled "We're Queer, Remember?" "Liberationist, like liberal,
has become a term of abuse," he wrote. The oppressors are
everywhere in Warner's piece. As America's right has gone
further right, so the extremists of the gay left have gone further left. Old heroes of the gay liberation movement are now
trotted out like the enemies of the Chinese Cultural Revolution. Larry Kramer, the founder of ACT UP, Gabriel Rotello, a
committed left-winger, and Michelangelo Signorile, the
Prince of Outing, are now denounced: "Kramer saves his
most demeaning language for gay men who have sex or those
who, like Edmund White, dare simply to write about it. Others, like Gabriel Rotello and Michelangelo Signorile, claim to
speak for the middle. They, too, tell us to be less queer."

Kramer, the father of the modern liberationist gay
movement, experienced the intolerance of the gay left he had

helped create as he prepared to deliver his New York Gay Pride speech of 1997. Sadly, because of his own mistreatment of speakers he didn't like, he had to preface his remarks with a request: "Please don't hiss and boo." He concluded his speech by saying, "Well, there's never been a revolution yet where its instigators didn't get knifed in the back, usually by their own."

The assimilationists were still in firm command of the movement, and they were looking forward to the future. In 1997 at a gay ski weekend in Aspen, attendees heard Barney Frank and Elizabeth Birch compare Clinton to John F. Kennedy and Vice President Al Gore to Lyndon Johnson. Elizabeth praised Gore's sensitivity as well as that of his wife, Tipper. Later that spring, Gore defended television actress Ellen DeGeneres in her famous "coming out" through her character on the show *Ellen*. Dick Morris, Clinton's ex-advisor, explained Gore's comments: "I agree with everything he said substantively, but that is pander, pander, pander. . . . Gays are a huge source of money for the Democratic Party—that's why he's doing it. It's hurting him in the general election, probably even hurt him in the primary, and he's doing it because he needs to raise money. That is a pander."

"Don't Call Me an Activist"— The Gay Republicans

In October 1984, I sat on the couch in the lounge of Divinity Hall, on Divinity Avenue, after my first month at the Harvard Divinity School in Cambridge debating whether to tell the crowded room my secret. It was a tough decision I faced whenever I was getting to know new people. We were gathered to watch the debate between Geraldine Ferraro and Vice President George Bush. As the debate progressed, punctuated with screaming and applause for Gerry, I realized that no power on earth could have helped George Bush with my fellow classmates.

I was new to the school and to my fellow students, and I was overwhelmed by the whole place. I had come from a college and home where support for Reagan-Bush was a given, but my world was suddenly now upside down. I turned to the guy next to me and expressed my opinion that Mondale chose Ferraro in desperation, that Mondale was a goner. I was met with stony silence.

With a puzzled look, he asked the dreaded question: "Are you a Republican?"

I had outed myself. What should I do? Should I go along with the crowd and pretend to like Mondale? No, I couldn't stomach that. I could say that I was an Independent, a voter that swung both ways. I could get self-righteous and say that "I support the person, not party labels." But that wouldn't be completely true either. I was a Republican, a centrist Republican because of my libertarian views that the best government was less government, a firm believer in the power of individuals to organize themselves in free market economies. On the controversial social issues like gay rights and abortion, I felt the government really had no role. My Republican politics were an outgrowth of my sense of the best way America could govern itself.

I made the decision to be honest with my classmates

that day, to tell the truth and let the chips fall where they may. I came out as a Republican. This heretical view made me one of the least popular students at Harvard Divinity School over the next three years. Growing up in the American Baptist Church, I had experienced my share of right-wing ideologues, but I had no idea the left had its share, and they were just as intolerant, if not worse.

My classmates had gone to the best schools in the world. They'd studied history and economics, and met people from every walk of life. And yet many of them still supported Marxist revolutionaries in Central America and were intolerant of those who disagreed. I had to walk through a field of crosses for Salvadorans "killed with American bullets" each day on my way to class. The only time we prayed in my three years at Harvard was when a professor led the class in a prayer for the innocent children killed in the 1986 American raid on Libya. I remember his prayer went something like "O supreme being that is in us and with us" (for one could never say "God," and certainly not "the Father"), "we pray for innocent children killed by the powerful. . . ."

In my contrarian style, I asked if we also might pray for the innocents killed by terrorists. The reaction from my fellow students wasn't one of compassion. If looks could kill, I'd be dead.

In one mandatory seminar the theme for the term was liberation. We read liberationists of all kinds. The favorite for many of my classmates and professor was Mary Daly, a feminist theologian at Boston University. When I criticized her for her intolerance, I provoked tears among the women in my class. Through her tears, one classmate lashed out at me. "Those are the comments of a straight white male—the product of privilege!" she screamed.

I knew in that moment that if I pulled out my "gay card" I could probably trump her "woman card." Sort of like victim poker—a gay beats a white woman. But the whole game of victim trumping went on every day at Harvard and it made me sick. As a result, I just kept my mouth shut.

When I returned to class the following week, I was met by our male teaching assistant. He informed us as we arrived that the women in our seminar had decided that the class was no longer "safe" for them, and had voted to meet with the feminist professor separately. I turned around and walked directly to the dean's office and raised hell, and the class was forced to meet as a unit. That happened during my first term of my first year at Harvard Divinity School, and I didn't get any more popular.

Those on the intolerant left love to stand in solidarity with the oppressed, especially when their standing with them requires not a bit of sacrifice. I couldn't help using humor to make that point.

Jesse Jackson, speaking at Harvard's Memorial Church on the apartheid issue, cried out that "Harvard's hands were crimson with the blood of South Africans" for not "fully" boycotting the country. My fellow divinity students leapt to their feet with applause. Watching these privileged white students applaud such criticism made me think of a fun practical joke that created some accountability. I put up posters around the school with hands dipped in red paint imprinted all over them. The poster read: "Rev. Jackson is right. OUR hands are crimson with the blood of South

Africa. We call on all divinity students to stop accepting your financial aid until the boycott is complete."

I put some ridiculously long acronym at the bottom. Needless to say, the poster made students uncomfortable but they decided that they could take the tainted financial aid if they used that money to fight "the System." When they found out it was a joke, they expressed fury at my "insensitivity."

My three-year education in and exposure to the intolerant left was not without its positive side. I met some great people and worked at Harvard's Memorial Church all three years, under my mentor the Reverend Peter Gomes, a fellow American Baptist and Republican. Peter has the best response to the questions posed to Republicans by liberals. After he prayed at inaugurations of both President Reagan and President Bush, Harvard society was furious with him. At one of his famous dinner parties, a woman asked, "How could you do it? How could you?"

Peter asked her what she was talking about, and she explained, "How could you be a Republican? How could you pray for Reagan?" Peter responded, "Madam, my people were freed by Abraham Lincoln, and I haven't forgotten it." More recently when Peter was asked on a radio call-in show how he could be a Republican, he responded, "My family and I were Republicans when the current leadership were wearing hoods."

But just to show that God has a great sense of humor too, I ended my Harvard experience with a laugh. Our graduating class was gathered to choose two people as class marshals who would lead us into Harvard Yard on graduation day. A friend of mine shouted out, "Rich Tafel," which was met with snickers and sighs, but my name was entered into nomination, along with two others. After the three of us left the room, the class voted. I lost to the other two, and from what I heard it wasn't even close. The marshals chosen by the class were the guy who headed up the gay group and the woman who headed up the black group—a display of the power of identity politics.

However, a few days before graduation the dean called me into his office. One of the marshals hadn't fulfilled some academic criterion and wouldn't be graduating. I would need to fill in as class marshal. You can only imagine the looks on my classmates' faces when they saw that conservative guy lining them up to lead them to Harvard Yard.

Harvard Divinity's liberation theology had hit its apex when I graduated in 1987. Since then, the school has been moving back to the sensible center. But my experience there was good preparation for the ideological intolerance I would encounter within the gay community's restrictive world of identity politics. My experience in coming out as a Republican, I would learn, was a common one among gay libertarians. In the same way that I was "out" as a Republican before I was "out" as a gay person, libertarian gays have often established their positions on the size of government, the importance of the individual, defense issues, and the role of the free market before they have gotten around to declaring their sexual orientation.

The whole idea that I needed to fear coming out as a Republican demonstrates the bizarre intolerance of the left. Why would I forfeit all of my worldviews on foreign and economic policy simply because identity politics assigned gays to the Democratic Party? Why in the world shouldn't I remain in the Republican Party where I shared many views, and be out as a gay man? As I saw it, integrity required me to be an honest Republican instead of a dishonest Democrat. Gays, rather than flocking to comfort, need to demonstrate courage and their true diversity, coming out wherever they are regardless of whether others are comfortable or welcoming. It was becoming clear to me just how much therapeutic thinking and identity politics dominated the gay movement.

★

After I spoke about the importance of coming out in the Republican Party on a trip to San Francisco, one man asked the question I'm almost always asked. In a whiny voice, as he literally hugged himself, he asked, "I was raised Republican, but I don't feel *embraced* by the Republican Party. How can you be active in a political party that doesn't like you?" "I didn't get involved in politics to be liked," I replied. "I got involved because I believe in certain principles of individual rights, less government, and free markets—all traditionally Republican positions. I also hold certain values, and politics is the arena where our society battles for or against those values. I don't like the status quo within my party on gay issues, but I do have a vision of what can be, and I'm working for those changes." He just gave me a perplexed look. I added, "If you want to be embraced, get a boyfriend or a dog. But don't get involved in politics because you need a hug; you'll just get hurt."

During a presentation that Clinton appointee Bob Hattoy and I were making to a group of gay congressional staffers, Bob actually compared my work in the Republican Party to a woman who, for deeply pathological reasons, returns to her abusive husband for more battery. In his view, among gays, where the need to be embraced is so important, politics meant going where you are liked. He could only conclude that my working in a political party where there is homophobia must be a product of a deep masochistic desire. He couldn't comprehend that I don't care what they think about me or what he thinks about me—that I didn't get into politics for affirmation. He could not see that I was guided by principles, looking ahead to effecting change that would benefit every gay person. In fact, only when gays get beyond caring about what everyone else thinks will we move ahead in the political arena.

The audience members actually working in the trenches, almost entirely Democrats, had a healthier view of politics than Bob. One after another, they came to my defense. "If Rich is successful in making the Republican Party in any way more gay-positive, then my boss is more likely to be more pro-gay," one said. "If he can offer some negative fallout within his party when Republicans are bad on gay issues, that gives us some leverage with our bosses."

"When Republicans took over, I was really worried," another confessed. "I'm glad gay Republicans had some access." These gay Democratic Hill staffers understood that political strategy meant getting beyond being liked. They wanted results.

Working with Republicans on a daily basis also meant accepting them as human beings. Politicos often compare their political strategies to intimate relations. I was reminded of Barney Frank's defense of Michael Dukakis in 1988. He said that voting for Dukakis was a one-night stand, not a marriage. On numerous occasions, liberationist gay Democratic friends described Bill Clinton as leaving them feeling like a cheap date. These comparisons reflect the confusion of politics, which is the battle between ideals and power in the public square, and intimate personal relationships, which meet our deepest human needs. This confusion eventually leads to hurt feelings and almost total cynicism about politics.

I'll never forget the horrid response to the Colorado contingent during the March on Washington in 1993. Those poor souls had just gotten kicked in the teeth by losing the fight against the anti-gay Amendment 2, which sought to forbid the state from passing any gay rights laws and nullified those that had already been passed. Many bystanders decided that to remain in Colorado was a sign of weakness, and responded accordingly. So as the Colorado contingent marched by the throngs of onlookers, they were booed by their gay "brothers and sisters" on the sidelines. These gay Coloradans, who were on the front lines of the gay movement, were received with contempt by those who should have been applauding their courage. As if by not fleeing in the face of homophobia, they were somehow complicit in it.

When I kicked off the first meeting of the Indianapolis Log Cabin Club, attendees told me how they had to park their cars blocks away so no one would know they were gay.

The new president told a dramatic story of how he came out to his boss to be able to lead that night's meeting. This is the modern gay rights movement. Gay leaders in metropolitan centers, who speak mockingly of gay people in the South and Midwest (often where they came from), should realize that these people who are coming out in the South or Midwest, in the Republican Party or the Catholic Church, are the cutting edge of the gay rights movement—it is not in Washington's Democratic strategy meetings.

One can only imagine the gay politicos' response to the news that Rosa Parks had refused to sit in the back of the bus: "Why would she want to sit in a part of the bus where she wasn't welcome? She must just hate herself to submit to that abuse." Justice requires us to stand up for truth wherever we are. The more dangerous the place we make our stand, the more important it is that we stand up and come out. This is particularly true for gay people, because often until we come out where we are, no one knows we are there.

In a battle, you move your forces to the front lines. In today's gay political strategy, you are honored when you flee to safety. But courage in gay politics today is what it always has been: the willingness to go where you need to be, not necessarily where you're welcomed. For Harry Hay, it was America in the 1950s, and his own American Communist Party. Early gay organizing in the Democratic Party met with fierce resistance. Today, it takes more political courage to be an openly gay Republican attending a Republican conference or standing up to the far right in your party than it does to hold hands in Greenwich Village. We've got to go where the battle is, not where we want it to be.

Another damaging aspect of therapeutic politics is the need to demonize your opposition. Let's refer to this as the Fort Apache approach. Life in Fort Apache wasn't great, but if you complained, those in charge would point to how dangerous it was outside the gates. As long as Democratic leaders can point to evil Republicans outside the gates, gays are less likely to make any demands of their protectors. The demonization of Republicans and those who try to work with them has hindered the gay movement from moving beyond its liberal urban base. If Republicans were not seen as frightening, then gays might begin to question what they're getting from the Democratic Party.

I saw this clearly in a meeting of AIDS lobbyists back when Democrats controlled both houses of Congress. Whenever a Republican senator's name came up as someone in need of a visit, the activists began to hoot. "I didn't wear my pearls today," laughed one lesbian activist, "so I'll let someone else lobby the Republicans." A gay man in attendance responded with great camp: "I didn't wear my heels! Sorry, find someone else."

This mocking of Republicans might make gay or AIDS activists feel self-satisfied, but it accomplishes nothing for people with AIDS. When Republicans took over control of the House and Senate, gay and AIDS activists who had for years demonized them and refused to meet with them could only predict disaster. Only Log Cabin had access to key Republicans, and we were pleasantly surprised as Republicans showed a greater response to the AIDS crisis in their budgets than in those proposed by the White House. In 1997 alone, I visited almost every Republican Senate office, and found that most of them had never been visited by any gay or AIDS lobbyist other than Log Cabin's.

The assimilationist and liberationist branches of the gay movement find American politics more and more frustrating because the therapeutic view limits their idea of politics. The therapeutic attitude says each autonomous individual is valid in making his or her own meaning—logic lies in "whatever makes you happy." But this radically individualized morality, devoid of any civic sense, leaves little room for political debate in the public square; just feelings remain—"and feelings can't be wrong."

The breakdown of the politics of feelings that we are now witnessing within the gay community is paving the way for new modes of thinking that could slowly overtake the political movement. Gays and lesbians are rejecting the pigeonhole of identity politics. They are refusing to accept the image of being victims or suffering from oppression. They are changing their perspective and demanding to be out wherever they are.

The primary requirement of the gay political strategy for the next century will be to understand the difference between fulfilling personal needs and political needs, between the desire to be liked and the desire to be free. Gays need to stop demonizing those within their own community with whom they disagree. Gay libertarians have been shunned and driven out of the gay movement because they've refused to compromise their complexity. This is a great loss. The coming generation of gays is eschewing the pressure to fit in, neither pretending to be straight and remaining in the closet nor pretending to be Democrats when they are not.

★

I was at a forum in South Carolina during a presentation at one of the Renaissance Weekend gatherings, a retreat for leaders in American public life, when I found myself sitting next to a high-level figure in the Clinton administration. After I responded to his query as to what I do, he smiled and said with a laugh, "Must be pretty lonely." Jokes about gay Republicans abound. "Do you hold your meetings in phone booths?" and so on. But the myth of the invisibility of gay Republicans is shattered during election cycles.

In 1988, 40 percent of gays voted for George Bush. In 1992, following the disastrous and virulently anti-gay Houston convention, half of the gay Republicans who voted for Bush in 1988 bolted the party for Clinton. That year, Bush took the lowest gay vote ever recorded for a GOP presidential candidate, when only a hard-core 12 percent voted Republican, which still compares favorably with the Republican vote of every other minority group that year. In 1994, the Republicans ran on the libertarian Contract with America, which brought 33 percent of the gay vote to congressional Republicans—a far higher percentage than the vote from any other minority. In 1996, after Bob Dole returned a Log Cabin check, apologized for doing so, and made the first ever specific promises on gay concerns (which I'll discuss in detail later), he received 25 percent of the gay vote. In 1998 one third of gays voted Republican. But the gay movement has done everything it can to keep up the impression that all gays vote Democratic when, in fact, they are the highest-voting minority group for the GOP.

Libertarian gays find their political home in either the Democratic Leadership Council wing of the Democratic Party or in the libertarian or moderate wing of the Republican Party. The more that the Democratic Party moves away from a reliance on big government solutions, while at the same time the Republican Party embraces a big government moral agenda, the more gay libertarians will find themselves in the Democratic Party. At this time, most libertarians still find their home in the Republican Party, finding it the better choice for their beliefs in individual rights, individual responsibilities, less government, and free markets. Gay Republicans have found themselves on the front lines of a debate on the future of the GOP with those in the religious right who would like to see the Republican Party be an actively anti-gay party.

Surveys show that gay Republicans are generally more likely than their Democratic counterparts to be entrepreneurs, are more likely to live outside gay urban centers, are more white, male, and profoundly more religious than the assimilationists and liberationists. Gay Republicans are independent thinkers and their voting patterns are more similar to those of straight Independents than they are to conservative Republicans or gay Democrats. Gays in the Republican Party often get criticized by the so-called nonpartisan gay establishment for being too partisan; but voting records show that gay Republicans are the least knee-jerk, partisan voters in the gay community, and are more likely to vote for the person, not the party.

Most gays who identify as Republican do so because that party best represents their view of individual rights, responsibilities, freedom, and economic and foreign policy. Many gays who remain Republican refuse to accept the victimization they see in the Democrat ideology. Gays who held more traditional beliefs about religion, American democracy, capitalism, and even political parties were coming out and finding the sometimes anti-American, anti-capitalist dogma of the gay leadership foreign to them.

Gay Republicans, finding nonpartisan groups inhospitable, slowly began to organize their own efforts in the late 1970s and early 1980s. In San Francisco, a group of gay business leaders organized Concerned Republicans for Individual Rights. In Chicago, CARGO (the Chicago Area Republican Gay Organization) was established. In Seattle, Gay Republicans of Washington (GROW) was formed. And in Los Angeles, a group of gay Republicans started the first ever Log Cabin Club in 1978. There were numerous attempts to pull the gay Republicans together in the 1980s. At the 1987 March on Washington, gay Republicans tried forming a national organization under the name United Republicans for Equality and Privacy (UREP).

★

Gay Republicans are not a new phenomenon. Alex Wentzel's story is interesting because he speaks for many who, like

Dorr Legg, have been around since the founding of the movement, but have for the most part remained invisible because they don't fall into the assimilationist or liberationist camps.

Alex became a political junkie at the age of fourteen when over the radio he heard a voice crackling from the floor of the 1940 Republican convention. "Mr. Chairman, Alabama, the cradle of Dixie, proudly casts its votes for the next president of the United States." The Republican nominee was Wendell Willkie. Alex remembered that "the intrigue of horse trading for support and smoke-filled rooms made the drama of politics exciting.

"Gay rights was not the burning issue for me when I registered to vote in 1947," he said. "In fact, I didn't really know what being gay was or whether I was gay myself. But I did have a consuming interest in Republican Party politics." Like many libertarians, he had his ideology in place before he came to grips with his sexuality. But his coming-out experience still puts him among the pioneers of the gay movement, and it is all the more interesting because he views his coming out in terms of Republican politics.

"During President Eisenhower's second term, I came out to myself as a gay person, remaining, however, deep in the closet," he said. "This was not a time of open understanding of sexual orientation. The isolation of the period made it difficult to come to grips with yourself. Little or nothing was available to read about homosexuality, and that which was available was unsupportive and very judgmental."

Alex chose Texas as the place to settle and to begin establishing his gay life.

"I found an excellent position as a statistician at an electronics company," he said. "But even better, I met a wonderful guy named Dick Anderson at, of all places, a Valentine's Day party. He became my life partner—we've been together for thirty-eight years."

Typical of many libertarian gays, Alex had an entrepreneurial spirit and a strong sense of public and private life. "We [he and Dick] later became business partners in a furniture/interior design business we ran for fifteen years. Those were wonderful years, but we were very careful to keep completely separate, discreet worlds between our public image and our personal, social lives. Most of our social life revolved around very private house parties."

In 1982, after retiring to California, Alex Wentzel did pioneer work in forming the local gay Republican club. "I had really never felt connected with the political work of the gay community," he said, "as it was so Democratically oriented. I attended the first organizational meeting of the Log Cabin Club of Orange County, and was amazed how many other gay Republicans there were." Like Alex, many gay Republicans I talked with found Log Cabin the first place where they could feel comfortable in gay politics.

Alex became the first president of the Log Cabin Club of Orange County in 1982. For a man who treasured his privacy, the media attention he received was jolting. "As soon as the press got wind of the story," he remembered, "that an honest-to-gosh gay Republican organization had formed in Orange County, the bastion of ultra-right-wing Republicans like Congressmen Bill Dannemeyer and Bob Dornan, my quiet retirement was ended. Reporters showed up on my doorstep for interviews and photos. My neighbors had the opportunity to read about my new position on the front pages of the *Los Angeles Times* and *Orange County Register*, with my picture prominently displayed.

"I told Dick to be prepared for anything, as we were still in uncharted waters. One Sunday morning, the phone rang at 7:30. It was someone I had never met, thanking me for doing something he wished he'd had the courage to do himself. As an employee at a local aircraft company, he couldn't risk his security clearance by joining Log Cabin, and he just wanted to say thank you. He never gave me his name, but he did give me a very warm feeling about the work we were beginning. None of the expected hate calls materialized. No graffiti was painted on our doors. In fact, one neighbor who I drove to the veterinarian when her dog was hurt actually commented: 'You are the big celebrity of the neighborhood.' I was never prouder of myself for taking this big plunge."

Alex watched with great concern and confusion as socially conservative Democrats became Republicans and began taking over the California Republican Party. He never understood why the right was so obsessed with the lives of gays and lesbians. In an article, Congressman Bill Dannemeyer claimed that homosexuality was a sin. GOP state assemblyman John Lewis said it was a sickness. "It occurred to me that they'd better get their act together," Alex remembered. "If it was a sin it couldn't be a sickness and if it was a sickness, it couldn't be a sin."

In the early 1980s, Alex pioneered putting a face on gays within the Republican Party. He and Dick Anderson went to visit the chairman of the Orange County Republican Central Committee, Tom Fuentes, who refused to support Log Cabin or even attend a meeting. It was a frustrating experience, but Alex learned the power of taking a stand and organizing by being a politely in-your-face gay Republican, simply by being himself.

"My first Republican state convention was not encouraging," he recalled. "Vicious anti-gay rhetoric was heard in committee meetings and on the floor. It was intimidating. On Sunday, I was awakened by the press calling to get my response to Congressman Bob Dornan's attack on gays at a prayer breakfast that day. As the reporter read his comments, I kept telling myself to keep my cool and be articulate. I couldn't just shoot off my mouth, as I was representing the entire Log Cabin Club. So I responded rationally and with dignity, which is more than can be said for Dornan. It also occurred to me that for the first time Bob Dornan would not go unanswered. Log Cabin would always offer the balance that the gay groups of the time were never able to do."

Frank Ricchiazzi, who came to be known fondly as the godfather of Log Cabin in California, came to understand politics in the Democrat-controlled city of Buffalo, New York. Growing up in a working-class Italian family, Frank remembers kneeling at the local Catholic church alone and crying, staring up at the crucifix begging for some insight as to why he was attracted to men, why a loving Christ would put him through so much pain. Following service in Vietnam, Frank wanted to be a banker in Buffalo and got some good advice during one of his interviews for a job: "Get out of Buffalo and go west; there aren't going to be any good jobs for anyone here. Staying here will be a dead end."

California's anti-gay Briggs Initiative of 1978 politicized Frank. "Log Cabin Los Angeles can thank State Assemblyman John Briggs for getting our club formed," he said. "His initiative, which would have banned gays from teaching, brought more gay and lesbian Republicans out of the closet than anything to date and led to the creation of Log Cabin Clubs in California."

Immediately, the local Republican Central Committee chairman called a meeting with the club, which was then known as the Lincoln Club, and asked it to change its name. The local party had already named its top donor group the Lincoln Club. As a result, there were some early, comical mix-ups in which some of Los Angeles's most prominent citizens would brag that they were members of the Lincoln Club. Frank and his colleagues enjoyed the fun, but agreed to change the name, and in keeping with Lincoln they chose Log Cabin.

In 1982, Frank took another pioneering step for the gay community, running for office as an openly gay Republican in the California legislature's 55th Assembly seat. While he didn't win the race, he put Log Cabin on the political map in California in both the gay community and Republican Party. Running as an openly gay Republican in 1982 was no picnic, Frank remembers.

"The day before the filing deadline, the chairman of

the Republican Candidate Development Committee called to tell me that someone else had also filed. However, he went on to assure me that I had nothing to worry about, and that he personally would ensure that the party would help me out."

"This other guy's a member of the Log Cabin Club," the chairman told Frank. "You know what that is, don't you? They're just a bunch of faggots, they're all disgusting people. Don't worry about it, you have nothing to worry about because we will never let those people win." Frank was stunned. The chairman had confused Frank with the other candidate.

"After that call, I began to realize that I was about to enter ten months of hell," Frank said. "I was afraid, and beginning to realize that to run as an openly gay Republican candidate would be a very lonely haul. I would have loved to have seen the chairman's face when he realized that I was the 'faggot.' That operative avoided me at every Republican meeting for many years to follow. He could never look me in the face, and I made a point of locating myself near him."

While Frank received little support from the Republican establishment, the voters were different: "They were uninterested in my sexual orientation. They cared about our country, our economy, and our foreign policy. They are kind, considerate, hospitable, and generous. They saw me as an individual they could trust. I enjoyed campaigning in this district."

But Frank's greatest shock came from the response he received from the gay community. "Naively, I expected that the gay and lesbian community would be thrilled to have an honest-to-goodness, openly gay candidate running for office in this district. My naïveté was immediately shattered by my early lesson about gay politics. I quickly learned that there is no such thing as a nonpartisan gay political action committee. The groups in L.A. were completely dominated by a left-leaning Democrat mentality."

He described the Municipal Election Council of Los Angeles (MECLA) as the gay powerhouse of its day, and a precursor of the Human Rights Campaign Fund in Washington. Frank describes how the Democratic Party "stroked MECLA, took their money, patted them on the head, and sent them on their way. Needless to say, their funds went almost entirely to cultivating Democrats."

Frank received neither an endorsement nor funds from MECLA for his race. To his surprise, "they gave no money to any primary candidates, with the exception of one—my opponent." Even David Goodstein, the publisher of the *Advocate*, made a pitch for Frank at a MECLA meeting: "I know this is going to come as a big surprise to many of you, but gay people do live east of La Cienega Boulevard. And, please brace yourself for this, many gay people are Republican."

Despite getting no support from the gay community and the brush-off from the Republican Party, Frank continued to organize even after the election. He looks back at his campaign experience with only positive thoughts. "One of the most important goals that my campaign achieved was the visibility it gave to the gay Republican movement, and particularly to the L.A. club. Many gay campaign workers told me it was their first time getting involved with a gay candidate or issue. Quite by accident, I discovered my candidacy had offered a role model to a generation of upcoming gay activists."

Years later, in 1990, Frank would be the guest of President Bush at the signing of two different bills in the White House—the Americans with Disabilities Act and the Hate Crimes Sentencing Enhancement Act, both gay-supportive bills. For the first time ever, a president had welcomed gays into the White House, and he was a Republican.

★

At the national level, Republicans realized that the identity politics of race and gender had locked all the various minorities into an informal New Left Democratic coalition. Their response was to tap into the opposition, especially among Southern whites opposed to black equality, while maintaining a hard line on Communism and fiscal policies to unite them with their Northeastern and Midwestern base. So while gays had achieved great success in 1980 by being permitted to address the Democratic convention, Reagan was eyeing the very constituency of Southern whites that Carter had awakened in 1976, which had been energized as well by the campaigns of George Wallace in 1968 and 1972. Reagan's Republican Party would take a dramatic step toward embracing this constituency during the 1980 general election, and, as a result, change American politics for a generation.

The same Pat Robertson who had gotten his feet wet in politics by campaigning for Carter in 1976 switched parties and endorsed Reagan in 1980. Many viewed the United States during the Carter years as victimized and defeated. Because most Americans did not see themselves as a nation of victims, many conservative Democrats began switching over to the GOP. On the other hand, fearful of being in a party with Southern social conservatives, many Northern Republicans considered dropping their party labels and registering as Independents or Democrats.

By 1984, Republicans, who had written off minority groups to the Democrats, began the first ever use of very subtle gay bashing. The Democrats held their convention in San Francisco, and Republicans labeled Democratic nominee Walter Mondale, Carter's liberal vice president, the leader of the "San Francisco Democrats," San Francisco being famous as the mecca for gay lifestyles. The code worked.

The list of Democrats who switched to Republican in the 1970s and 1980s is a Who's Who of America's far right, including Pat Robertson, Texas senator Phil Gramm, and the eventual Republican Senate leader, Trent Lott of Mississippi. Reagan himself, a former Democrat, made it easy to switch with his often-used expression: "I didn't leave the Democratic Party—the Democratic Party left me."

In 1984, there was an effort to organize the gay Republican network within the Reagan administration under the name Concerned Americans for Individual Rights (CAIR). After a well-attended first meeting in McLean, Virginia, one small item about the meeting in *The New York Times* terrified most of those who were involved, and scared away potential members.

★

Hal Gordon, a gay man who worked as a speechwriter for the Reagan administration, doesn't remember much anti-gay rhetoric inside the White House in those days, although there was some: "Like the day a colleague of mine introduced me to a new staff member: 'He's one of us, Hal—not some quiche-eating fag!' I'll never forget that comment, but on the whole, my experiences were positive.

"I always felt that Reagan got unfairly cruel treatment from the gay community," he recalled. "Activists won't mention this, but I remember as far back as 1978 when Ronald Reagan declared that homosexuality is not a contagious disease, like the measles. I remember in 1984, President Reagan's response when he was asked where he stood on a pending gay rights bill during a nationally televised press conference: 'Let's just say that I am opposed to discrimination, period.' "

Like most gay Republicans, Hal saw his sexual orientation as something private, but finally decided to begin to come out to his colleagues: "I remember the warm response of those straight Republican friends that I confided my sexual orientation to, one by one."

But coming out at the White House has a formal tone to it too. Hal looks back with gratitude at his chance to come out officially during a security clearance interview.

"The White House security office avoided directly asking me if I was homosexual; however, in the course of one of my routine security checks I felt morally bound to make a full disclosure. So I took a deep breath and told them.

"I'll never forget that moment. I had somehow managed to choke out the words 'I am a homosexual' to the White House security officer, and yet the gilded roof did not cave in, nor had the marble floor given way beneath my feet. No avenging angel had struck me down. I still had a job, and my career was intact.

"If anything, the officer was rather blasé about the whole matter. He thanked me for my candor, and assured me that I had done myself more good by owning up to my nature than by attempting to conceal it. He was right. My security clearance came through a couple weeks later, and with it came the promise that I would have absolutely no problem obtaining a higher-level clearance in the future if I needed it. Maybe the weight of the world wasn't lifted from my shoulders when I finally came out, but the accumulated strain of leading a double life for twenty years certainly was. Every public action I've taken as a gay man since then stems from that single experience. It struck me then that no one in the gay political organizations had the ability to begin the discussion with the Reagan administration about homosexual equality. After expending all their efforts to help Democrats, no gay activist should have been surprised that homophobia is a problem in the Republican Party."

Upon graduating from Vanderbilt Law School, Bob Kabel went to work for Republican governor Winfield Dunn of Tennessee, first as his liaison to the Tennessee congressional delegation and later as his scheduler and liaison to cabinet members. After the governor's term expired, he moved to Washington to work for a Republican senator from Arizona, Paul Fannin. Later he became legislative director to another Republican senator, Richard Lugar of Indiana.

In 1986, President Reagan hired Bob as his liaison to the Senate. During his clearance process, the fact that he was gay and in a long-term relationship didn't come up. After leaving the Reagan administration, he was nominated by Reagan as a part-time member of the Foreign Claims Settlement Commission, and was confirmed by the Senate, all without any reference to his sexual orientation. Bob was clearly a Republican who was coming to terms with living as an openly gay man; he operated under a "don't ask, don't tell" policy of his own. His circle of friends included mostly gay Republicans with a few friendly Democrats, but almost all had dealings on the Hill.

The recently formed AIDS Action Council, a nonprofit AIDS lobbying group, held policy group meetings in Washington, with local, high-powered gay Republicans, including Bob, to assist in developing a strategy for dealing with the Reagan and Bush administrations and congressional Republicans. Bob gave money to AIDS causes, and when he was introduced to an AIDS Action staffer by the executive director as "one of our Republican supporters," the staffer replied, "Oh, I'm sorry to hear that." Five years later, when the Log Cabin Republicans were organizing a national office, Bob, now a partner at a prestigious Washington law firm, found a place to participate. He was elected chairman of the board.

★

As I've shown already, the AIDS movement's early leaders were for the most part a product of the gay movement. In the AIDS movement, you will find the same three categories: liberationists (ACT UP), assimilationists (AIDS service centers), and libertarians (unorganized, but volunteering). In this crisis, the gay establishment's responses range from fearful of big government when the issue is mandatory testing or quarantines, to embracing of big government when the issue is socialized health care. Liberationists at every stage of the AIDS crisis have called for "queer" sexual freedom against the system. Meanwhile assimilationists call for a benevolent government to sweep in and care for AIDS "victims" in every facet of their lives.

Key to AIDS politics was ensuring the victimization of people with AIDS, which wasn't difficult to do, as societal and government apathy were very real. Not until the disease spread beyond the gay community did the general public get concerned. Discrimination against gays was so prevalent that many people with AIDS had to pretend they had some other, more acceptable disease. A joke at the time went, "Did you hear about the guy who got AIDS? Now he's got the tough job of convincing his parents he's Haitian."

The gay left's ability to blame Reagan for AIDS has been so embedded in the gay community's collective mind that it helped suppress gay Republican organizing. It is rare when I speak to a liberal gay audience that someone doesn't bring up Reagan and AIDS. In February 1998, I spoke to a gay community breakfast in Broward County,

Florida. During my speech I shared the success Log Cabin had achieved on AIDS issues in the GOP Congress, with historically high funding increases. Still, in the question-and-answer period one questioner got up and started yelling about Ronald Reagan and AIDS, demanding I apologize for Reagan. I responded by making the point that President Reagan didn't veto any AIDS bills, because the Democrats never offered one at any time while he was president. Reagan had been out of office for a decade and the current Democratic president, after six years in office, hadn't kept his promises on AIDS issues. Meanwhile, even though the Republicans were showing real leadership on AIDS, many still chose to focus their anger on them.

★

The pundits have joked that the 1992 Republican National Convention in Houston was better in the original German. But for gay Republicans it was a turning point. In the same way that John Briggs's anti-gay initiative helped build up the Log Cabin Clubs of California, so did Pat Buchanan help create a national Log Cabin movement.

Many gay Republicans, who had for too long rationalized the closet, were enraged by the Houston convention. As one longtime Republican staffer described it to me, "I've given my life for this party, writing bills, speeches, and strategy. I didn't tell them I'm gay, because I thought it didn't matter. Now, after Buchanan's speech, they say it matters, and I'm mad as hell."

Kevin Ivers, then a twenty-four-year-old legal librarian

from Washington, D.C., and an organizer of the Capital Area Log Cabin Club, remembered the Houston convention as the turning point in the organizing of gay Republicans.

"Houston was horrific. Pat Buchanan, who loyal Bush supporters fought against in every Republican primary, was given a prime-time slot to speak," he recalled in his journal. "That speech, full of lurid and violent references to an emerging 'cultural war' in America, left me feeling sick. My sense of patriotism had been wounded. He meandered from one deeply disturbing image to the next, painting a picture of a nation on the verge of civil war over an insolent refusal to tolerate difference.

"It was the speech that followed that should have redeemed the evening. Ronald Reagan strode out to the podium and delivered perhaps the best speech of his career. The moment was steeped in history, as everyone knew in some way that we were seeing the Ronald Reagan we knew and admired, the man who unified a party of stark contrasts and led this country like no other president, for probably the last time. He spoke confidently and warmly, undaunted by age.

" 'Whatever else history may say about me when I'm gone,' Reagan said, 'I hope it will record that I appealed to your best hopes, not your worst fears, to your confidence rather than your doubts.'

"Reagan's contrast to Buchanan was sharp," Kevin went on, "and I remember fighting back tears of disappointment and exasperation while the hall filled with howls of adoration for the old man. After traveling the many roads to Houston through the 1992 campaign, the driving sense of unified purpose embodied in Ronald Reagan was draining away in that hall for too many people. What was happening to this party?

"I believe that the gay Republican 'movement' was truly born at that moment. With Log Cabin, we had taken a discordant national organization and redefined it as a group dedicated to a singular message of pride and principle. Nothing would unleash the creative spirit of gay Republicans more than that evening in Houston. And never had I felt the hand of God more strongly on my shoulder, pointing me in an unmistakable direction." Kevin would go on to staff the first national Log Cabin office in Washington, where he serves as the director of public affairs today.

Marty Keller, an openly gay alternate delegate to the convention and Log Cabin member, found that horrific convention a turning point for himself too. "Never before had it been so clear to me what it meant to be a gay Republican," Marty said, "and how important our role in the GOP and in the debate for the future of our country was. Our role was to belie the rhetoric—if gays were the problem for America, then the GOP could no longer pretend that they were immune. Our presence at that convention and our Log Cabin convention in Houston a few days earlier made it clear that the Republican politicians could never again refer to the 'San Francisco Democrats' or 'out-of-the-closet liberals' as a coded anti-gay attack. We were gay and we were Republican. How was Dan Quayle going to explain that to America?"

Alex Wentzel described Log Cabin's nonendorsement of Bush this way: "I'd been a registered Republican for forty-five years at that point, and while I did not always support Republicans, I never had voted for a Democrat. This time the Republican Party left me no choice. From the outcome on election day, I knew I was not alone in that perception."

★

I was living in Boston in 1992 when I received a call from Marvin Collins, a friend of President Bush from Texas, who once chaired the Texas state GOP. "Bush is going to lose. If we're going to ensure that we don't have another convention like this in our party, we need to raise money and open a national office in Washington. If you can find the person, I'll help raise the money to get it off the ground." And so, the national office of the Log Cabin Republicans was created from the words of Pat Buchanan.

The younger grassroots leaders of Log Cabin at that moment shared a devotion to Ronald Reagan. While gay Democrats had successfully demonized Reagan as nearly the principal cause of AIDS, young gay Republicans who came to their political sense outside of the gay community emerged in the gay community with an already established view of American politics and Ronald Reagan.

Bruce Carroll, a member of the Philadelphia Log Cabin Club, typifies the Log Cabin sentiment: "I grew up as a Republican, yes, a Reagan Republican. I still have a soft spot in my heart for Ronald Reagan, the president I grew up with. But these days I probably have an ideological connection closer to Colin Powell and Christie Whitman. I am sometimes frustrated, sometimes angered, and sometimes hurt by the Republican Party. But I have never given serious thought to fleeing my party because I relate closer to the overall core views of the Republicans than to either the Democratic Party or any other political organization out there today."

Bruce's political poise comes in handy. On a gay chat bulletin board, Bruce, like many gay Republicans, has been called a "Jew working for the Nazis." "That comment is so typical of the anger which prevails when those who claim to speak for the gay community encounter anyone who strays off the appointed path," he said. "That type of anger is no different than the inexcusable words of the religious right. The left-leaning gay activists and right-wielding moralists unite together in their tactics of squelching free speech and opposing views on a subject."

Michael Aronowitz is another activist anchored by Ronald Reagan's example. He grew up on Long Island in a middle-class family with a Catholic mother and Jewish father, and at age thirty served as president of Log Cabin Republicans of New York City, the Northeast regional director on the national board, and spearheaded the effort to create a statewide Log Cabin organization in New York. His comments about Reagan are typical of the young leadership in Log Cabin: "When I was growing up, Ronald Reagan made me proud to be American. It's that simple. National defense is really important to me. If we can't protect ourselves, then what else matters? I'll never forget how Reagan stuck to his guns on SDI and outspent the Russians. The greatest issue in my lifetime was the end of the Cold War."

With his love of country and respect for Reagan, he found the 1992 convention devastating: "I was furious at the Houston convention. Bush ceded the party to nothing less than hatred. Then they stuck Reagan in the late hours after Buchanan. I could never vote for Clinton, so I voted for Ross Perot. I'm absolutely convinced that the hatred they preached drove people away from their TV sets and our party."

Michael is one of the most tenacious and successful leaders in Log Cabin, organizing new clubs, raising money, and cultivating close working relationships with New York Republicans such as New York City mayor Rudolph Giuliani, former senator Alfonse D'Amato, and Governor George Pataki. Within a year of his rise to a top position in our organization, he became one of the most well-connected gay activists in New York. The secret of his success is simple to him: "I think we've been successful in New York because the political leaders are really interested in liberty for all people. I treat them with respect, and I think they respect our politics. Many gay leaders spend way too much time vilifying Republicans. They lost the chance to have clout in the GOP, and I don't think they can be trusted by the GOP."

He remains worried about the future of the party: "If the Republican Party is going to lead this country, it is going to have to capture the middle. Clinton's doing it. We need to shed the radical right."

Gay men are not the only ones who feel squeezed between the values they hold and the Republican Party's attitude toward their sexuality. Very few lesbians identify themselves publicly as Republicans. The gender gap that the Republican Party faces with women is worse with single women and even worse with lesbians. Ninety percent of lesbians affiliate with the Democratic Party and half of those rate feminist issues of more importance than lesbian-specific issues.

The courageous story of a lesbian Log Cabin member (I'll call her Pam) and her involvement in Massachusetts politics offers some sense of the difficulty of being a lesbian Republican. Raised by her parents to believe that hard work pays off, she grew up to embrace the concept that one had to contribute to society in order to reap its rewards. Conservative when it came to the national debt, she came to resent the values offered by the welfare state and the personal inertia it fostered.

At the same time, she developed more libertarian positions about the role of government in the lives of women: "I grew convinced that the debate over abortion was more a question of power than a question of when life began. I didn't trust the motives of the fundamentalist right. I believe they are reacting to their perceived loss of power. I concluded that abortion was the vehicle for them to reassert their power. And this power was represented in draconian proposals such as forbidding abortion after a woman had been raped. This became humanly real for me when a friend of mine from college was raped. She was Catholic and sought support from her church; instead she received only rejection. This crystallized my belief that a woman's choice is more than protecting her right to choose, it is about empowerment."

Her libertarian politics, however, served to restrict her social options, and she found herself thwarted in her attempts to enter into a meaningful personal relationship. The women she met, while educated and intelligent, were unwilling not only to accept her conservative beliefs, but to honor her right to hold them.

Whether it comes from the left or the right, however, Pam sees little difference in the intolerance people display. "The teasing I took for my politics reminded me of the teasing I took growing up, and it struck a raw nerve. Being different is tough, and there was always something sort of different about me. I was too skinny, too smart, too athletic, too obedient, but never just called normal, or okay. My self-esteem took a beating, and I internalized much of the criticism."

The rise to power of the religious right has made her less comfortable in the Republican Party. "My social values are less and less welcome in the Republican Party. I guess this is how bisexuals must feel at times, unwelcome in either camp. Because of the self-confidence I gained from my family and my natural inclination not to simply follow, I find myself as a political Lone Ranger sometimes. Friends have asked me why I don't just become a Democrat, where I'd be welcomed as a lesbian. Others have suggested I should join a third party. I've considered those options, but I've decided that I'm not involved in politics to feel good. I'm involved in politics because I believe strongly in this country, and I want to make a difference—for the better. The Republican Party today is the place where lesbians and gays can make the biggest difference. Most gays and lesbians feel that because the Republican Party is weaker on civil rights issues, we should not join it. But why should I compromise my fiscal beliefs in the Democratic Party?"

Seeing an ad for Log Cabin Massachusetts, she decided to see what these gay Republicans had to offer. But on arrival she experienced the discomfort many lesbian Republicans feel in male-dominated gay Republican meetings. Her unease abated, however, as she began to talk with individuals there and found that not only were they welcoming, but they even expressed excitement that she was Republican. "They were all interested and supportive to hear from me firsthand the travails of being a lesbian Republican. This marked the first time I had ever been in a gay setting where people truly wanted to know what I thought about politics. The welcome I received was a pleasant surprise. It means a lot to anyone when we meet people who appreciate us for who we are, and I enjoyed the support."

Eventually she became comfortable with her own complexity: "I finally stopped caring what people thought of my political views. I actually now enjoy telling women that I'm a lesbian Republican. When gays and lesbians fully accept themselves, and ourselves as a community, then maybe others will do the same. We need to practice what we preach about diversity, and allow each gay person's contribution to mean something. When we move in this direction, we are on the road to becoming a community that will make a historic difference."

Steve May is one of a growing crop of openly gay Republican candidates running for and winning public office.

At twenty-six, he was the youngest member of the Log Cabin Republicans board of directors. Raised as a Mormon, and having served in the military, Steve had a conservative upbringing. Running for the Arizona House of Representatives, Steve is also comfortable in his complexity, and his integrity is gaining him many supporters. I was struck by the conversation Steve and I had with Arizona Republican senator John McCain, who told him after the loss of his first race: "Don't be a quitter, you've got to run again." In his first race, Republican and gay leaders both opposed him because neither side felt he represented the party line.

In 1998, May raised $17,000 in one evening, the highest for any challenger in the state. When a local gay paper asked him why he was Republican, he answered: "I don't think that when I come out as a gay man, I have to change my political registration or philosophy.... While most Americans have difficulties understanding homosexuality, they believe that homosexuals should be treated fairly under the law. And most Republicans believe they should be treated fairly under the law too."

To a gay community that is spoon-fed identity politics, where so-called gay issues must dominate all other issues, May cedes no ground: "The gay community shouldn't be misled into thinking that I'm going to be some kind of full-time gay rights activist in the legislature, because I will not be. I'm planning to work on issues of growth, education—specifically the funding of education in public schools—and also public safety. That's the banner I'm carrying."

How Gay Republican Strategies Can Advance the Gay Equality Movement

Perhaps because they do not feel they represent the bulk of gay voters, gay Republicans have been reluctant to lead within the gay movement. But that has so far denied the gay community the most powerful political idea: libertarianism. The information age is uniquely tailored to the libertarian strategy, and the signs are everywhere. Libertarian ideas of strong national defense, free markets, individual rights, individual responsibility, and limited government are gaining new acceptance, but, more to the point, these are ideas that are compatible with and conducive to happy and integrated gay lives.

Strong National Defense

One of the issues that has attracted many gay people to the Republican Party is its traditionally vigorous support for a strong national defense. Given the choice between a candidate for president like Jesse Jackson who is supportive of gay rights and another candidate who has a weaker position on gay rights but supports a strong national defense, many gay Republicans would vote for the person who they feel will offer the greatest basic protection to all American citizens. On the face of this, it would appear that gay Republicans are voting against their own interests, but the gay Republican views his interest as an American citizen in danger of having his country invaded as outweighing the need for passage of a gay rights bill. In other words, what is the point of having a president who supports domestic partnership but at the same time would leave the country vulnerable to an invasion from an outside enemy?

I think that generations of gays who lived through the Cold War and who chose the Republican Party based their decision on the belief that foreign policy and national defense were of paramount importance. As the fear of attack from outside forces has subsided, so has the importance of this issue lessened as a primary reason for gays to be attracted to the GOP. In fact, the Cold War allowed the GOP to pull together a diverse coalition of voters on social issues who were united against Communism and who prioritized that issue when they voted. The fall of the Soviet Union served to unveil the divisions within the GOP on social issues, many of which had emerged only over the previous two decades, for example, abortion and gay rights.

Arthur Collingsworth's story is a common one in showing how many gay Republicans of his generation chose the Republican Party. Collingsworth got involved with Republican politics because of his views on foreign policy. Few gay people could describe a more horrible rejection than Arthur. As a teenager in a Michigan public school in the 1960s, he was caught by members of the faculty while engaged in a gay relationship with a fellow student. Branded a deviant by his teachers, he was brought before the entire student body, where male classmates were warned to stay away from him. His adoptive parents declared that they were embarrassed to have taken him in. With no opportunity to be accepted on any social level, Arthur escaped into books. The only members of the faculty who extended any help to him were a few librarians. Years later, it occurred to Arthur that those same librarians were probably gay themselves.

Through his reading, he developed a great knowledge of the world. Rather than respond to rejection with rage, attempts to reshape himself in a heterosexual mold, or even suicide, Arthur created a fanciful world in which he saw himself as an expert on international affairs. As a teenager, he drew on his already considerable knowledge of world affairs and wrote to world leaders commenting on their actions. When his letter arrived on the desk of the president of Brazil, someone there saw a public relations opportunity.

The government of Brazil flew Arthur to the country to get his insights and to discuss his ideas. The U.S. Information Agency contracted with an American film company to produce a documentary on the visit—*A Midwestern Boy Writes to the President of Brazil*. Arthur was named Correspondent for the Brazilian Government Trade Bureau to Michigan and Ohio, and took his mission very seriously. He celebrated his fifteenth birthday in New York City at a lavish party hosted by the Brazilian consul general. Arthur had gone from outcast to celebrity on the power of his ideas. He eventually parlayed all of this into a scholarship through college and a fellowship for graduate school.

His understanding of world affairs led him toward the internationalist and strong-defense positions of Republican politics. In graduate school at Georgetown University's Department of Government, Arthur became an adamant supporter of Richard Nixon in his presidential race against

Vice President Hubert Humphrey in 1968. When Washington newspapers reported on the likely rising stars of the Nixon campaign staff, Arthur was highlighted. Then one of his colleagues gave him the news that he would be passed over for advancement because he was gay. Devastated by this injustice, he vowed never to return to politics.

Arthur did, however, remain a lifelong Republican, and in that capacity he went on to become a premier international fund-raiser. Remembering the life-changing benefits he had attained through his trips to Brazil as a young man, he devoted much of his time to fund-raising for international student exchange programs. After six years of service as an official of a United Nations agency, he also chose self-employment rather than the hardships of political life. In 1993, when the Log Cabin Republicans were in the process of establishing a national office in Washington and organizing the group's corporate structure, Arthur joined the board of directors and was elected treasurer. He lobbied senators and members of Congress, many of whom he had met over the years through his international work. He even met with old friends at the Heritage Foundation, a leading conservative think tank, all of whom he knew from his anti-Communist days. This time, however, he was counseling them against gay bashing.

Free Markets

My friend César from Colombia had been in the United States for six months when the annual gay pride parade was held in Washington. I'm not a big fan of gay pride parades, where some people feel the need to broadcast all of their personal preferences from the back of a flatbed truck. But my jaundiced view of the parade was ameliorated when I saw it through César's eyes. He had questions about everything. We laughed at the campiness of many of the participants, and the desperation of some to reveal their specific personal sexual desires. As group after group marched by on 17th Street in Dupont Circle, the "gay strip to the fruit loop," as it's known, César wanted to know more about all he'd seen that day. Coming from a country that has a gay rights law, but where being gay means sneaking out to bars and even having to maintain a spouse for public appearances, César was curious about why the United States, which does not have a gay rights law, allows personal freedom for gays, while his country does not. The difference between the two countries is our free market system.

The ability to own our own businesses, spend our income where we want, and work in a free market system has allowed us to succeed in ways that have not been available to gays in other countries. The fact is, America's business community is far ahead of America's legislators in offering employees nondiscrimination. And a quick look around the globe shows that where there are free markets, there are freer gay people, and where markets are less free, gays have fewer civil rights. Free market economies, with their emphasis on the bottom-line success of companies, create a greater opportunity for employees to be judged on their performance and not on their personal lives.

One would think that this relationship between free markets and free people would be obvious to the gay and lesbian community, but that's not the case. In the last couple of years I've had the opportunity to speak before an audience of grassroots liberationist activists at "Creating Change," a conference hosted by the National Gay and Lesbian Task Force. Each year I've begun my comments by articulating Log Cabin's support for individual rights, individual responsibilities, less government, and free markets. And each year, when I've said "free markets," the audience has booed and hissed me.

I've found myself and other gay Republicans repeatedly caricatured as being wealthy. I've been told that I'm a Republican because I'm rich and want to protect my money, though in truth I come from a family of eight and we were comfortably middle-class suburbanites. Most gay Republicans I've met, especially those who are wealthy today, came from lower-income families. Their hard-won success in attaining the American dream has led them to the GOP.

Some gay Republicans come to the party from their experience with the success of the free market, while others come from their bad experiences with the politics and economics of the far left. Dennis DeCoste's story is an example of both. Dennis grew up in a lower-income family in the federal housing projects of New Bedford and Gloucester, Massachusetts, and he learned the hard way about the role free markets play in creating more freedom and justice for the individual. One of his most vivid childhood memories was when Sears repossessed his mother's washer and dryer.

"As she stood crying while the crew removed the machines, I stood looking up at her feeling utterly helpless," he said. "I vowed then and there that I would have more financial security for myself and those I loved."

An excellent student, Dennis got a scholarship to Harvard, where he became part of the growing number of students in the country who were becoming increasingly uneasy about the escalating war in Vietnam, especially as his college draft deferment expired. In the midst of this great social upheaval, he also became increasingly involved in some of the most radical elements of the anti-war movement at Harvard, joining Students for a Democratic Society (SDS), and later enlisting with the Maoists, "Little Red Books and all," and the Progressive Labor Party (PLP).

Today he looks back with humor on that period of his life: "It was the whole nine yards: dictatorship of the proletariat, aligning with China against the Soviet Union." He learned how the left took power, and put the methodology to work. Through political maneuvering his small band of two hundred PLP members was able to take effective control of SDS with its much larger membership (thirty thousand).

Dennis also came to understand why both young people and those with inherited wealth would be drawn to the New Left: "In the foolish glow of youth and idealism, this preposterous theory of governance can actually seem promising for society's downtrodden. My experience tells me that this theory is most appealing to social elites. I myself was one of the very few members of the PLP at Harvard that was actually from a blue-collar background. But I soon got to see firsthand the fatal flaw of Communism. To succeed it requires a political organization that ruthlessly suppresses any and all forms of opposition, from within and without."

Dennis turned away from what he describes as the "moral bankruptcy of the left." "I left Communism for the gentler, kinder left wing of the Democratic Party. My stay was short. In the course of watching President Jimmy Carter self-destruct, I concluded as do most ex-Communists that only free market capitalism is a viable environment for social progress and justice, imperfect as this environment might be. The alternatives are all worse."

Dennis spent the next seven years teaching elementary school in Boston's ghettos, and then decided to go to Stanford University's business school: "I decided to hitch my star to high-tech start-ups in Silicon Valley. I've done eight start-ups since, creating thousands of jobs, billions of dollars in shareholder value, often changing the way the world works and lives. It is a dream come true. And, so far, no one has taken away the washer and dryer."

Dealing with the personal, Dennis returned to the political as a board member of the Log Cabin Republicans. "Much of my activity to support Log Cabin is motivated by the thought that if we can make the Republican Party a more perfect, libertarian-style party, the lives of future gay persons and leaders will be easier. The Republican Party has a long way to go. But from the day I accepted Harvard's scholarship I have never forgotten the words of one of my interviewers: 'You will be expected to give back in your life what we are giving you today.' From that moment I knew I had accepted a solemn duty. I am giving much more of my time and money to Log Cabin than I had ever expected to, but I consider my work in the gay community as part of my solemn duty to make this world a better place."

Free markets have moved beyond national economies to a global economy. Today, even the former Soviet Union and Communist China, once shining lights for liberationists, are themselves struggling to allow free market capitalist reforms. The positive reality of these changes is everywhere, yet the gay liberationists remain hostile to free market capitalism, as is demonstrated by the hissing I receive at the National Gay and Lesbian Task Force's conference every year.

I commented that I'd have an easier time convincing my fellow Republicans that gay rights were consistent with individual rights than I'd have of convincing this audience on the value of free markets. The audience nodded in agreement. Many gay activists aren't simply dismissive and unaware of the importance of free markets—they are absolutely hostile to the idea. For them, the capitalist system remains oppressive to workers and to the poor, and they believe that true justice for gays and all oppressed peoples lies in overturning that system, not working within it.

Gay individuals are already thriving in the information age, most notably in the competitive American workplace. The more competitive the industry, the more gay-supportive the companies. Already more than half of the Fortune 500 companies in America have established nondiscrimination policies for their gay employees. It is no accident that Silicon Valley leads the nation in corporate gay-friendliness. They simply don't have time to play games with what their employees do in their personal life; they must by necessity embrace diversity or lose their competitive edge. They need to make a profit, and that means they need brains, creativity, ambition, and contentment among their employees, an environment ideally suited to the openly gay person. Another example of the move toward simply accepting talent however and wherever it is found can be seen in the fact that 50 percent of employees in the technological field are immigrants.

A look at the map also confirms the connection between free markets and gay freedoms. Where a section of America has been drawn into the industrial age for a longer period, that region is more gay-supportive. Rural and agrarian America, with its mores of the core extended family unit, isolation around village life, and emphasis on procreation, remains the hardest place to be openly gay today. In the industrial heartland, there are a smattering of gay businesses and gay groups trying to organize. And the locales quickest to embrace the explosive free market of the information age, such as California's Silicon Valley or Route 128 in Massachusetts, are by far the most gay-supportive locations in America. The same correlation applies in the international community as well.

Failure of the gay movement to understand the power of free markets has also been detrimental in the fight to find a cure for AIDS. In the 103rd Congress, when socialized health care briefly seemed to be a done deal, I wrote an op-ed for the *Washington Times* opposing such a move based on the impact it would have on the free market incentive for scientific advancement, particularly in AIDS drug development.

Two years later, after the Clinton administration's efforts at price controls were rejected, the private sector, driven by the profit incentive, developed and produced breakthrough, life-saving drugs for people with AIDS and put them on the market. The death rate for people with AIDS has plummeted. People with AIDS are alive today thanks to our free market economy. Yet ACT UP celebrated its tenth birthday in 1997 by criticizing through protests the companies that had developed the best treatments for AIDS for making too much money on drug sales. Each year, activists introduce some effort to impose government price controls on AIDS drugs, apparently without the understanding that if they were successful, they would be destroying the incentives necessary to save lives.

This is not a choice between either no government involvement or total government control. The role that the activists see the government playing is in placing controls on the prices of drugs. Then, using those savings, they want the government to spend much more on the rest of the health care structure. If this were ever fully acted on, the result might be more funds available for patients to buy drugs, but chances are there would be fewer drugs available.

In a more free market–based model, the role of the government would be to get a discounted rate for patients who don't have health insurance. In addition, Congress would provide funds for drugs for those relatively few individuals who are without insurance and who don't qualify for Medicaid. This model encourages drug companies to produce more AIDS drugs, because such a decision is profitable.

The free market forces of capitalism which gay activists so deride are the very forces that have permitted us to organize and thrive and, in the case of AIDS, to live. As global markets become free markets, the gay movement's continued opposition to them hinders our advancement toward more freedom. Global market trends indicate that in the future the gay movement of the First World will be joined by gays in the developing world.

Individual Rights

In the spring of 1997, I was in the studio of the all-news cable channel New York 1, about to join a debate on the record of Republican mayor Rudolph Giuliani. The news of that day for gay New York politics was that openly lesbian state assemblywoman Deborah Glick had been passed over in favor of a heterosexual black woman, Virginia Fields, when the Democratic mayoral candidate, Ruth Messinger, made her endorsement for Manhattan borough president.

Gay Democratic activists were furious. Ultraleft, openly gay then–City Council member Tom Duane said that he was tired of giving money and votes to the Democratic Party and getting nothing in return. A liberationist leader from ACT UP, Bill Dobbs, called it "the meltdown of the gay leadership" in New York politics.

When I was asked to comment, I said, "It was the meltdown of gay identity politics." What struck me most about that debate was that no one made any reference to the merits of either candidate. The New York Democratic machine was so mired in special-interest identity politics that all it could think about was not offending one group more than another. Identity politics has forgotten the importance of individuality—both candidates were simply symbols in the city's spoils system.

At the same time gay political leaders tell the straight society that they demand respect for diversity and demand that gays should be judged as individuals, they have punished those in the gay community who act as individuals. The wing of the Democratic Party that embraces identity politics views people not as individuals but as members of a group. This kind of identity politics too often forces members to suppress their individualism, and too often requires groups to trade on their victim status.

I experienced the use of victim status at my first ever national gay organizational meeting for an effort to plan the 1992 March on Washington, which I mentioned earlier. The discussion leader spent the entire first half of the day deciding how we would come to decisions. She drew laughs when she said, "I guess only the gay Republicans would be happy with Robert's Rules."

An early proposal of the group was that women and people of color be given the right to veto all group decisions, as they were underrepresented that day and had been disenfranchised by the patriarchy for so long. An outspoken black gay Republican jumped to the mike.

"If we're going to allow those underrepresented groups to veto anything, we must also allow gay Republicans to veto, as we are underrepresented here," he shouted. The audience responded with nervous laughter, and the veto concept was scuttled.

The crowd had planned on holding the march in April

1992, during the presidential election campaign, but that plan drew opposition. A Native American lesbian named Hatchet pointed out to the crowd that Native Americans and other "progressive" people planned a major march in 1992 to commemorate "Christopher Columbus's rape of America." She challenged white gay men to demonstrate "gay, lesbian, bisexual, and transgender" support for the oppressed Native Americans and not conflict with their march.

One participant suggested that the seating for the meeting, which was set up in a theater style, had been arranged in a male, patriarchal manner, and moved that we form into a circle, much like an encounter group. No one objected. As the discussion progressed, someone suggested we pass around a crystal, popular in New Age therapy, to each person as he or she spoke. This would "focus the speaker's energy and the group's energy." I was finally up close and personal with therapy instead of politics, political correctness instead of strategy, and the power of identity trump cards.

Hatchet, it appeared, was winning the day with her plea for solidarity with the victims of Columbus, and the consensus moved toward holding the march in 1993. But the black Republican again broke the consensus. He grabbed the mike.

"Where the hell were the Indians in our march of 1987?" he shouted. "When was the last time Indians stood up for gay rights? This is silly, and I think we should hold our march in 1992 like we planned!"

The circle sat in shocked silence. Finally, an Asian-American got the crystal.

"What I have just heard pains me a great deal," he said. "To hear that kind of speech from a fellow person of color is doubly painful." In a melodramatic gesture he walked to the center of the circle, fell to his knees, and said: "We must call it when we see it. That was racism, pure and simple, and it makes it very painful for me and many of us to continue this discussion."

The outspoken gay Republican again stood up and replied, "You're calling me a racist? Let me tell you about racism." At that point our happy, crystal-passing circle fell apart.

The moderator suggested that all people of color leave the room to meet separately and discuss the pain of what had happened, and return with their feelings. I couldn't take it anymore, and left shortly after the caucus in the hall.

On my way out, I walked past the group whose feelings had been hurt, as they stood in the hall. They were linked arm in arm, and each person in turn was explaining what people-of-color group he or she represented. I waited to hear the one white guy in the circle explain his credentials: "I'm Bob, and I date Latin guys, and the comments inside were painful for me, too."

This comical story of my first national meeting with gay activists reflects the dominance of group victim rights instead of individual rights within the gay movement.

★

Log Cabin San Antonio member Robert Blanchard came out at fifty-five after living for years in the closet. He discovered the new intolerance of identity politics facing him as he entered the gay community. His rejection of victimization politics is one of the most common threads running through the stories of gay Republicans I meet.

"I soon discovered that, although I was a newly liberated gay man accepting full responsibility for my life, my search for integrity and integration was immediately challenged by the political hegemony of the gay left. The gay liberationists tried to assign me two new roles—one as victim, the other as recovering oppressor."

In a recurrent theme among gay Republicans, Robert's core Republican principles of individual rights and individual responsibility were not the norm in the gay community he was attempting to be a part of. Instead, he was encouraged to view himself as a victim. "To be a victim, I would have had to give up my newly achieved sense of personal responsibility. I would have replaced it with a perverse comfort in my powerlessness. When one's decisions have few actual consequences, one can do whatever one pleases."

He encountered a new rigidity very much along the lines of what Dennis DeCoste encountered in his days as a Communist at Harvard. Blanchard doesn't mince words: "Worse yet, the left's doctrinaire, identity-politics orthodoxy, replete with speech codes, would not allow any dissent or even discourse about its commitment to a narrow, nongay, bankrupt political agenda, reflecting a blind, ideological commitment to biological determinism, group identity, group autonomy, and resistance to assimilation."

Most politically active gay Republicans got involved with Log Cabin only after being frustrated in their attempts to get involved with technically nonpolitical, nonpartisan organizations. At the national level, organizations such as the Human Rights Campaign and the National Gay and Lesbian Task Force appear much more intent on aligning themselves with Democratic Party politics than even attempting to work honestly with Republicans. When I first began lobbying Republican members of Congress on Capitol Hill, the vast majority had never been visited by anyone from a gay organization before.

"I found that the Log Cabin Republicans provide a venue where individual responsibility is a value," Robert said. "I found a forum in which I can openly explore and express my individual and complex views about economic and political issues. Both at meetings and casual social events, discussion and debate is protected in an environment of openness and civility."

As a gay Republican in Texas, Robert soon discovered that the fight for individual rights needed to be waged on two fronts—the gay left and the religious right. He's been part of a statewide effort to take back the party from the religious right: "Log Cabin members and chapters directly challenge and engage the theocratic right-wing toe-to-toe, eye-to-eye in precincts, district conventions, and state and national conventions. It is ironic that the gay left conflates the Log Cabin Republicans with 'the right.' "

As Robert's observations indicate, group identity manifesting itself in the identity politics of the Democratic Party is stifling the growth of a complex, difficult-to-label, and wonderfully diverse gay community. I have yet to attend a meeting with other gay leaders at which identity politics doesn't play itself out. At one town hall meeting, a Latina lesbian, angry because there weren't any Latinos on the panel, charged from the audience, labeling each person on the panel with great contempt. "Women of color!" she pointed. "White Republican," she announced. "Men of color," and down the line, "White women!" As if all you need to know about anyone is his or her ethnicity or party affiliation.

One reason the far right has succeeded in successfully calling gay rights "special rights" is that so many of the supporters of gay rights really support special rights for other minorities. Openly gay journalist Jonathan Rauch, who wrote "Kindly Inquisitors: The New Attacks on Free Thought" for *Reason* in 1993, predicted the rise of the special rights campaign of the religious right: "What the right has figured out is that if you can frame someone as a special pleader, a special interest in America, that person is rightly in trouble." The gay community and many throughout the country are so wedded to special rights legislation that offering another paradigm won't be easy. The fact that much of the opposition to these laws comes from people who don't want gays to be treated fairly has only strengthened the appeal of gay rights laws within the community.

Gay Republicans find themselves divided when it comes to support for employment bills that protect gays from being fired, bills such as the Employment Non-Discrimination Act (ENDA), which is currently being pursued in Congress. They ask themselves, how can a person be in favor of passing another nondiscrimination bill and at the same time claim to be against big government? The truth is that I actually participated in the drafting of ENDA, hoping that my input would make it a less intrusive bill than it might have otherwise been. For example, I pushed for language that would ban affirmative action for gays, and while many on the drafting team support affirmative action for other minorities, they agreed to make it clear that that result was not what we were looking for.

The reasons for supporting ENDA apply on a number of important levels. On the purely political level, the fact is that in 1964 America decided on how it would deal with disenfranchised blacks by adding a new law, the Civil Rights Act. A libertarian today might argue that the decision to move forward that way was wrong, an argument Barry Goldwater put forward at the time. But that same libertarian would have to acknowledge that this is the way our country has decided to protect minorities who experience discrimination in the workplace and in housing.

Today in America, if you as a minority are not on the list of protected groups, you may have no defense against discrimination. There are numerous documented examples from around the nation of gays who have been fired from their jobs and of employers who concede that they fired them simply because they were gay. Yet, when those individuals go to court to level charges of discrimination, judges tell them that they are, in fact, not protected under the current law.

The strategic reasons that national gay organizations have chosen to push for passage of such a bill is pragmatic. Protecting gays from being fired appeals to basic American ideas of fairness—an overwhelming number of Americans

support a federal law protecting gays from being fired simply because of their sexual orientation.

The less philosophical and more psychological reason
for employment bills could best be described as symbolic.
There are a few ironies here. The gay person who is most
likely to lobby for and support ENDA is likely to be a person
who doesn't live in fear of losing a job because he or she is
gay. The people most likely to need protections in the workplace are those who aren't out. The other irony about
nondiscrimination laws is that they usually pass only after
the majority of society is comfortable with the group seeking protection.

The symbolism of this particular piece of legislation
isn't lost on Capitol Hill. Both those who oppose and support ENDA do so largely as a measure of their own ideas as
to whether or not it is acceptable to be gay. Yes, they will all
wrap their explanations for support or opposition in philosophy, but at the end of the day their position on the bill
is their way of saying they support or don't support gay
people.

Gay people also tend to use bills such as ENDA to
track their own progress. If it passes in Congress, gays will
feel victorious, members of the religious right will feel defeated, and the country will experience a new climate of opposition to everyday discrimination in the workplace.

ENDA is a case study of the various levels at which civil
rights laws play themselves out in our society. I think we all
wish that gays could simply be given the same protections
everyone else is given under the Constitution, but until
that really happens, even gay libertarians will support legis-

lation that guarantees that we're all judged on our merit on the job and that no American is denied the same opportunity as another in trying to make a living. And before he passed away, even Barry Goldwater supported ENDA.

Author Andrew Sullivan is one of the few gay authors who understands the trend toward the individual and less government. He advised the gay community in *Virtually Normal* to shift its focus from seeking government protection to removing government-imposed barriers to equal treatment. He argues for a new movement strategy: equal marriage rights for gays, lifting the ban on gays in the military, and the repeal of sodomy laws.

The movement away from group identity politics toward a respect for individuals in all their complexity is growing. This is the perfect opportunity to show clearly where government and society still discriminate. And while the gay leadership is slow to change, there is a grassroots movement away from big government solutions on issues such as gay marriage, gays in the military, sodomy repeal, adoption rights, and the responsibility of being a good citizen.

Individual Responsibility

The AIDS epidemic brought out the gay community's best and worst impulses toward individual responsibility. No community in modern times has responded to its own needs better than gays during the early years of the AIDS epidemic. Friends and lovers suffered and supported one another through the devastation and death, while society

in general was either purposely neglectful or outright dis-
criminating. But the epidemic also took a toll on a community that had politically rejected individual responsibility
and embraced victimization.

David Clement of New York City, who sits on the LCR
board of directors, calls the gay leadership's response to
AIDS the "Big Lie." Growing up in a lower-middle-class Italian family in Plainfield, New Jersey, he was the first in his
family to go to college, which he had to pay for himself. After graduating, he served in Vietnam, for which he was
awarded the Bronze Star and the Purple Heart. "I served
happily in Vietnam, because I was welcomed everywhere I
went by the Vietnamese," he remembers. Through the G.I.
Bill, he was able to get his MBA at the University of Hart-
ford.

David lost most of his closest friends to the AIDS crisis, which led to a conflict of emotions—anger at the disease and anger at his friends for dying. For David holds
to another value of the libertarian-thinking gay person—
self-reliance.

To this day he remains angry at the missing element of
individual responsibility in gay politics. "I saw a community
leadership who weren't articulating any values. There were
no leaders. There wasn't one leader telling it like it is. For
years, the gay movement had been pushing the Big Lie.
They were denying what was so true. We were killing ourselves. Ronald Reagan and George Bush didn't infect gay
men with AIDS—gay men infected each other. Every gay
man that died of AIDS was infected by another gay man.
This is a fact, and no leader would say it. I kept asking my-

self, 'Where are your values?' It was dishonest for gays to never talk about personal responsibility in spreading AIDS, and then they turn around and say the government has got to solve it, to fund it—after we transmitted it! Where is our responsibility?"

Clement tried to plug into the local gay organizations. "I got to sit through a program where we blamed Republicans for all of our troubles. I kept hoping to hear some leader talk about taking responsibility for ourselves." He adds, "I remember the gay magazines saying three lies: First, that they can't prove it's transmitted by sex. Second, it's okay not to get tested, because there's nothing you can do about it. Third, it is Reagan's fault. The Big Lie was that the government must solve this—government must save us. How many lives would have been saved if one leader had the courage to say we can stop this ourselves?"

As an accountant, David saw the impact of the lack of individual responsibility in the lives of his clientele. "I watched some of my clients who were just a mess. They were making good money and just destroying their lives with drugs. Those that succeeded in pulling themselves out of it did so because they decided to change their lives. Those who waited for someone else or the government didn't succeed. I realized that government can't take care of you, you've got to take care of yourself. You've got to take responsibility for yourself, but too many in our community were waiting for someone else.

"My life changed when I accepted the fact that I was okay, that I should trust what I know is true for me. Once I trusted myself, my life changed, including my business life.

But everything I had heard from the gay movement was don't trust yourself."

Though it was an unpopular group in New York, David decided to take an active role in the Log Cabin Republicans. "I got involved in Log Cabin because I just asked myself, 'If not me, then who?' When LCR had an op-ed run in the *San Francisco Chronicle* calling on gay men to show individual responsibility, especially that we should be careful not to infect one another during sex, I know it sounds weird, but I just burst out crying. For the first time I saw leadership on a moral level."

David's call for a gay community that embraces personal responsibility is winning the day. Speaking to a group of five hundred gay and lesbian business leaders in Atlanta, I was asked a question about the status of a gay federal employment bill. "How can you expect us to come out when you still haven't passed ENDA?" was the question. I responded, "Employment bills will only pass when enough of America has worked with openly gay people next to them and that prejudice evaporates. But you can't wait for forces outside yourself to take control of your destiny. You must show courage and come out now. The next generation of gay people will benefit from it and so will you. And if you do lose your job because you're gay, I am sure that there are hundreds of people in this room who will hire you." I was pleasantly surprised by the applause that followed.

A gay movement that talks only about rights and about getting rights will always be rebuffed by society if rights are not wedded to responsibilities. An AIDS movement that talks only about government solutions and funding, without demanding personal responsibility for behavior, will find it very difficult to lobby for AIDS dollars in the coming generation.

On a very personal level, taking responsibility for your life means that you have some control over your destiny. Accepting victimization, seeing yourself as oppressed, means that someone or something outside of yourself controls your destiny. This key difference runs like a huge divide between liberationists and the assimilationists who see power outside themselves and libertarians who see power within themselves. The failure of a person to accept responsibility for his behavior can be debilitating, and even self-destructive.

Limited Government

David Warren was born in a lower-middle-class, secular Jewish neighborhood of Brooklyn in 1963. His upbringing was difficult. When he was nine his father died, and he was raised largely by his grandparents, who died a few years later. School life wasn't any easier: "The smart Jewish kids all took tests and then were bused to the good schools. I tested poorly, and remained in a school where almost all of my fellow students were black. They used to beat the shit out of me, partly because I was white and also because I was a nerd."

School was tough for other reasons too. "My mom knew I was dyslexic, but she didn't tell me or my school because she was afraid I'd get stuck in special education classes. I was such a nerd that I really threw myself into politics. My great hero was Gerald Ford, who united the country and saved the economy, and did it all quietly and never got credit. He lost because he pardoned Nixon, which was good for the country, but not for him."

Even in high school David worked on political campaigns: "I campaigned for Ford and Bush. I was nervous about Reagan the first time, but he won me over by 1984." David was no country-club Republican. "I'd been working as a concierge at an apartment building. I didn't make much money, but it allowed me to spend my days working on Republican campaigns. I was so poor then that I only had enough money to buy a can of sardines to eat on the subway each way to Republican headquarters."

As David got more involved with Republican politics, he also became more aware of his sexual orientation, and the two didn't fit. He loved Republican politics because it called for less government, but he saw contradictions too. He recalled the day in 1986 when the Supreme Court handed down the *Bowers v. Hardwick* decision, which concluded that homosexuals could be arrested for consensual sodomy, even right in their bedrooms, without a shred of constitutional protection. The ruling had a profoundly negative impact on the gay movement, and on David's life.

"In 1986, two things happened to me. I was trying to get involved with the gay community, but didn't fit in. I was more at home with the Young Republicans. The day *Bowers v. Hardwick* was announced, it really hurt my feelings. I felt there wasn't a place for me in America, and I loved America. I felt like that ruling meant America had no place for me."

Trying to take action, David attended a gay political

meeting. The group decided that they would protest the Supreme Court decision during the Fourth of July celebration at the Statue of Liberty, where President Reagan would light the torch of the newly restored symbol of American freedom.

"I went with them, and it tore me up to watch the gays waving signs in front of the tourists. One of the tourist families had come all the way from Los Angeles—with their kids and everything. And the gays were screaming at them. I was so embarrassed that I ran up to the tourists and apologized.

"I was so upset, I mean, I love America, but the *Hardwick* thing was just wrong. I felt sick, and I went to the gay community center to find a counselor, and then went to see Andy Humm, a local gay TV personality, but he didn't have time for me. He couldn't understand why I felt so hurt, why I loved America. And no way did they understand that I was a Republican. They were no help. I walked out of the gay community center planning my own suicide. I didn't fit in anywhere. I planned on jumping in front of a subway train."

He didn't go through with his plan, but life at home became even more difficult as his two worlds collided. "Guys would call me at home and my mom in her smoky, raspy voice asked me, 'Are these fairies calling you?' I told her that they were just Young Republicans, but she thought they had femmie voices. She asked, 'Are you a closeted homo?'

"I'll never forget at our Brooklyn Republican meeting one day—I was more and more gay, but no one knew—and then at one meeting there was a big, Irish Brooklyn-looking guy named Mike Flynn who stood up to speak. He got up among these very prejudiced, homophobic, mostly conservative Italian and Jewish Republicans and challenged them that they shouldn't be anti-gay. The Jewish woman next to me whispered, 'He's a fagala!' Mike became a hero for me, a role model. He was gay and conservative. I'd never seen that before. That was the beginning of my getting involved with gay Republican politics."

His early efforts to belong within a gay Republican group failed. "A guy named Bruce Decker and a group of gay Republicans were putting together a new organization in the late 1980s. I joined them for their meeting, and they ate a lot and drank champagne, and this was an expensive restaurant. I made sure I didn't eat much, just a bagel, because I only had thirty dollars to my name at the time. At the end of the meal, they divided up the bill evenly. I was too embarrassed to say I didn't have the money, so I gave my last thirty. I had to walk home to Brooklyn from Manhattan, and never returned to that group, which soon folded. I saved my money for the 1992 Houston convention, and met up with the Log Cabin group, where I finally felt at home."

Ultimately, David's reasons for becoming involved in the Republican Party reflect the fear shared by conservative thinkers of the gay Democratic embrace of big government: "I'm a Republican most of all because I don't like big government. I don't trust them. I think if government is too big and powerful it can do evil things. I didn't even like George Bush at first because he had run the CIA. I think we shouldn't give power to the CIA or FBI or any government agency—it is dangerous."

David's fear of big government is not shared by many

gay activists I've encountered. On the campaign trail in New Jersey for Republican governor Christie Whitman's reelection in 1997, I spoke before a gay and lesbian town hall meeting at Kean College. When I asked the audience if they believed big government could solve their problems, I got nods, smiles, and applause. The era of big government might be over for Bill Clinton, but not for that gay audience.

I then asked if they supported universal health care. Again, I got nods, smiles, and applause. Then I asked how they would feel if the health care system were under the control of Senator Jesse Helms or a Health and Human Services secretary named Pat Robertson. The audience shrieked with horror and began hissing. I replied that all the nose wrinkling in the world couldn't undo the danger of big government in the wrong hands. The big government gays build today can come back to haunt them tomorrow. No group should be more in favor of limited government than minorities, I said, because as history shows, no group is more likely to be abused by government than those in the minority.

In the early days of the AIDS epidemic the activists got a quick crash course in government regulation and protested at the FDA headquarters. But by the early 1990s the activist community had become the chief proponent of slowing down the approval of drugs through the FDA.

In 1994, Log Cabin AIDS advisor Jim Driscoll, AIDS treatment activist Jules Levin, and I filed a citizen's petition at the Food and Drug Administration to seek accelerated approval for the new generation of AIDS drugs. Contrary to the public perception, we encountered opposition to the early approval of these drugs from every major gay and

AIDS organization, on the grounds that the drugs were "rushed to market" for the sole purpose of making profits for the drug companies.

In fact, when the FDA approved 3TC, the first break-through drug for the new combination therapy, members of the leading elite AIDS organization, the Treatment Action Group, actually stood on their chairs in a hearing to voice their opposition to its approval. If these groups had suc-ceeded in their goal, thousands of people who have found new life after using the breakthrough drugs in combination would have been dead by now. The antagonism toward the free market from AIDS and gay groups can have deadly consequences for those we care about. When the FDA re-form legislation passed in 1997, with provisions to speed up breakthrough drug approval, Jim Driscoll was the only representative from either the AIDS community or the gay community invited to the signing ceremony at the White House.

In 1997, Log Cabin Republicans held its annual na-tional convention in Washington. It had been almost four years since we had opened the national office there, and we gathered only a year after the Republican National Con-vention in San Diego, where we had successfully prohibited any anti-gay speeches like those in 1992. At the Washing-ton convention, the highlight was the keynote address of Congressman Jim Kolbe, Republican of Arizona. He was the chairman of a House Appropriations subcommittee and a leading proponent in the Republican conference of NAFTA (the North American Free Trade Agreement) and free trade. He had also publicly come out just before we all went to

San Diego in 1996, and was at the time the highest-ranking openly gay member of Congress ever to serve.

His speech at the convention, which was broadcast nationwide on C-SPAN, was for many in the room a culmination of Log Cabin's work over the years. It was his first address before a national gay audience, and he chose the occasion to assault the big government mentality of the gay left and the religious right:

> I am both fascinated and amused by the convergence in views of some Republicans on the right side of our party with the views of gay, liberal Democrats. Neither would even admit their common philosophy, but it is there, nevertheless. The so-called conservative Republican deplores big government, welfare programs, erosion of personal liberties—and then votes for constitutional amendments to ban flag burning, or to proscribe specific medical procedures for a doctor performing an abortion, or to deny gays their rights to fully participate in our society.
>
> Liberal, gay Democrats, on the other hand, deplore the intrusion of government into the bedroom or the doctor's examining room—and then proceed to wax eloquent for programs that would nationalize the entire health care delivery system, or compel poor people to live in substandard housing operated by the liberal bureaucracy, or decry programs to give education vouchers to lower-income parents so that they might send their children to schools of their own choosing.

We might be pardoned for thinking sometimes that we are the only real Republicans around, consistently advocating smaller government and less taxes. We might be excused for excessive hubris for thinking Log Cabin Republicans are the only gays who really understand that individual liberties are for everyone.

The gay movement, which has until now focused on changing Washington, is beginning to realize the importance of limited government and the realization that real, lasting change takes place in the grass roots. This remains anathema to Washington-based groups that do their fundraising at the local level and pursue their politics in Washington.

Showing a disdain for the work of small clubs at the local level, HRC's Elizabeth Birch observed, "The Log Cabin Clubs don't amount to much," at a 1997 PrideFest talk in Philadelphia. These clubs, which had helped elect pro-gay mayors in the two largest cities in America, which had helped elect numerous city council members and governors, and changed forever the Republican politics of most of America's cities, didn't amount to much to Elizabeth because of her bias toward change emanating from Washington.

Today, Log Cabin remains the only gay political organization in the country with grassroots chapters working with a national office; to be successful, other organizations will need to follow that model. The demand for limited government means that power is spinning away from Washington, and gay power is boiling up from the grass roots, not down from Washington.

I witnessed the power of the grass roots when the Senate Labor Committee needed witnesses from the gay community for a 1997 hearing on ENDA. Log Cabin could immediately tap into our grassroots volunteer network. The coordinating Senate staffer, at a closed-door meeting with the principal participating organizations—HRC and Log Cabin—praised LCR's director of public affairs, Kevin Ivers, for turning up several excellent witnesses in so little time. She asked him how he managed to do it, to which Kevin replied that it only took an e-mail alert and a few phone calls to chapter leaders to find two of the three case study witnesses and one of the two religious experts. She then turned to the HRC staffers on the other side of the table, who had spent a year preparing for the hearing and had come up with a very narrow set of potential choices.

"Do you have chapters too?" she asked.

"We have dinner committees," one of them replied.

The success of the grass roots couldn't have been more apparent than when David Catania, a gay Republican, won a city council seat in Washington in 1997 and again in 1998. In a city with an eleven-to-one ratio of Democrats to Republicans, the national gay groups were astounded when he beat a Democrat in a head-to-head race. They had long talked about who would be the first openly gay Democrat to serve on the D.C. council. Rather than praising gay Republicans for the success, they responded with arrogance: "Catania may be gay, but his positions don't represent the gay community," said Kurt Vorndran of the Gertrude Stein Democratic Club, even though he conceded that most of his own organization's members voted for Catania.

The Challenge to the GOP

The Republican Party is at a crossroads. It can maintain the traditional tenets of the party of Lincoln: individual rights, individual responsibility, free markets, limited government, and a strong national defense. And it can invite anyone who believes in these core principles to join the party. If the leaders in the GOP choose this path it will become a strong, majority party that can offer true leadership to America as we fully enter the information age.

Or the GOP can pander to the religious right, which has gained some prominence in the party through its work in the local and state apparatus, not through any shared vision of the party's core principles. The Republican Party could reject its traditional tenets and adopt new core principles based on a fundamentalist Christian interpretation of the Bible. This would require new litmus tests that would cast out most elected GOP officials today. The GOP would require each Republican to be anti-gay, anti-abortion, pro–school prayer, pro-protectionism, pro-isolationism, anti–big business, anti-education, and anti-immigration. It would be a party that uses the power of a big, paternalistic government to impose an uncompromising social agenda on every American and every local community. Candidates who are divorced or who have admitted to drug use or adultery would be turned away; many who already control certain state parties, such as the party in Texas, are pressing to excommunicate any Republican who does not vocally support every comma and period of their extreme platform. If the party chooses this path, it will return to being a minority party with regional strength limited to certain communities in the Deep South and mountain West.

The gay issue in the Republican Party is simply the "canary in the coal mine." We are the first target of the religious right. The leadership of the GOP has gone weak on the threat the religious right poses, and in the growing vacuum of Republican leadership, as columnist Arianna Huffington said at the 1998 Log Cabin Republicans National Convention in Dallas, "various abhorrent fungal growths have blossomed." Any study of the religious right's advance, such as a thorough reading of *Active Faith* by former Christian Coalition leader Ralph Reed, reveals that its infiltration of the GOP is all about the acquisition of political power, not about some deeply felt affinity with core Republican principles. So when former House Speaker Newt Gingrich would spend one day announcing a set of bold, confrontational agenda items for the Republican Congress that focused entirely on core economic issues, and the next day emerged from a meeting, having been castigated by the religious right, to announce that the Congress would first deal with school prayer and abortion, it is no surprise that Republicans would scratch their heads and wonder in which direction the party was moving.

The party needs Republican leaders with the courage and vision to lead, not follow. Unity is forged by those who appeal to the most positive and uplifting values of everyone in earshot, not those who cynically play on the lowest common denominators of fear and division. The gay issue, perhaps more than even the abortion issue, cuts to the heart of this problem and stands as the greatest test for the future of the party.

So the choice for the GOP is clear and simple, not complicated. And whatever side you are on, one thing is for sure—it is not going away any time soon. Those who just put their heads in the sand hoping it will evaporate somehow will only find themselves forced into a corner. Bob Dole learned that lesson the hard way in his final campaign for the presidency.

"The Best-Traveled Cash in American Politics"

"The Log Cabin Republicans, whoever heard of them before?" joked Cokie Roberts of ABC News as she opened the 1995 conference of the National Gay and Lesbian Journalists Association. All of the top journalists on the panel with Roberts—from Al Hunt of the *Wall Street Journal* to Tim Russert of *Meet the Press*—were in agreement that the incident of the returned $1,000 check to the Log Cabin Republicans from the Dole for President campaign had changed the course of gay politics, and placed gay issues on the map for the 1996 presidential campaign. The leading writers from the gay and lesbian press throughout the audience, nearly all of whom were committed left-wingers, nodded in begrudging acknowledgment. This was the dominant issue of the panel discussion, a big news story that had a long history before it broke in the late summer of

1995. It was, many would say, the best $1,000 we never spent.

When moderate Republican friends call the LCR office in Washington on behalf of candidates that need help, I always try to oblige. After all, LCR's national office, where I go to work every day, was born of the hard-right turn of the Republican Party on social issues in the 1992 campaign. It was our charge, from the thousands of people who made it possible for us to do our work, to make sure that we never saw another Republican National Convention like 1992's again. So, as the 1996 campaign began heating up in earnest, I had a modest but challenging goal for our organization and for the GOP—prevent the gay bashing that pervaded in 1992.

When we were approached to consider supporting the Dole campaign, I figured it was a good opportunity to move closer to our goal. Republicans had just taken over the Congress, and gay and AIDS groups were filling the gay press with terrified prognostications, particularly on the future of AIDS legislation. The worst that could happen, I guessed, was that we'd support Dole, he'd lose the nomination, and he'd return as Senate majority leader—a valuable ally on important legislation. But I had to be as sure as I could that he wouldn't go anti-gay during the campaign.

At the first Dole event I attended, where I wrote a $1,000 check of my own, a friend introduced me to John Moran, Dole's finance chairman. He was interested in reaching out to Log Cabin. It was calculated that Dole had to raise more than $25 million to clinch the nomination, and people like John Moran spent little time with individual donors—he was looking for networks of people who could give the maximum dollar amount in short order. Gays already had a serious reputation for generosity in politics. A few months later, Moran invited me to the Dole campaign headquarters to discuss whatever stood in the way of Log Cabin and Bob Dole.

I went to that meeting very skeptical about the whole thing. Working on political campaigns had taught me to be cautious. During the meeting, I was frank about my chief concern—that Dole would pander to the anti-gay movement during the primaries.

"Do you want Phil Gramm to be our nominee?" Moran asked. "Bob Dole is an honorable man with many gay friends. He isn't a bigot. I'll be with him this week and share with him your concerns, but you have nothing to worry about with Bob Dole."

I explained that in addition to the assurance of no anti-gay moves, we would need something to energize our members in favor of Dole. The Ryan White Comprehensive AIDS Resources Emergency (CARE) Act, which was named for a young boy who died of AIDS after experiencing discrimination and which provided federal AIDS services, was scheduled for reauthorization in Congress in 1995. Senator Jesse Helms of North Carolina was promising to stop it dead in its tracks on the Senate floor. Dole would have to take Helms on and make sure the bill passed. The Ryan White CARE Act was Log Cabin's top legislative priority. Moran assured me that he would see what he could do.

Following the meeting, I was given a tour of the campaign, room by room, by one of Moran's finance committee members, who herself was a leading activist and financial backer of moderate Republican causes. She boldly introduced me as the head of the Log Cabin Republicans in every office and at every cubicle. At one point, a Dole staffer I recognized as a gay acquaintance—and there were many there that day I recognized as gay acquaintances—shouted, "I know you! I recognize you." When my hostess announced that I was the head of the Log Cabin Republicans, he turned bright red and blurted out, "No, I must have been thinking of someone else."

She turned to me a moment later and in a grand voice asked, "Is he . . . ?"

"Of course," I said. I thought it was obvious, but she seemed pleasantly surprised.

"We are running a diverse campaign here, aren't we?" she said, smiling.

After some follow-up correspondence and calls, we had clear assurances that the campaign would not do anything anti-gay. By putting our conversations and the follow-up in writing, the Dole people seemed to be indicating that they were were serious. Their support would be a monumental accomplishment in our party, given the dominance of the radical right in our primaries.

Word came to me from his office that Dole was preparing to join as a co-sponsor of the Ryan White CARE Act reauthorization bill—a public announcement to Jesse Helms that if he were to raise a finger against the bill, Dole was ready to fight. There was much elation in the Ryan White coalition when we let them know. And I knew we had to deliver on our end of the bargain.

I had been working to ensure that other Log Cabin members were turning up at fund-raisers in other cities. Moran would fax me advance listings of events and I would get on the phone and start twisting arms. Then, in June, a second, more elaborate, $1,000-per-person Dole fund-raiser was scheduled for Washington. I explained to the campaign that I would come on an LCR political action committee check, which meant our support would be public. They assured me it was no problem.

The event was chock-full of Republican House and Senate members, and I spoke to many of them with my "Log Cabin Republicans" name tag prominently visible. When I finally got a chance to talk with Dole, he nonchalantly read my name off the tag, thanked me for coming, and assured me that the Ryan White CARE Act would be voted out of the Senate in the next month.

"I know of your concerns with one of the members," Dole told me. "But we're going to work it out." I was impressed with his knowledge of our concern and this was the first indication that the leadership was ready to schedule a vote.

And, indeed, Bob Dole delivered. The bill came onto the floor despite Senator Helms's attempts to put a procedural hold on it. Then Helms started throwing amendments at it—five separate ones, each designed to gut or disable the bill in various ways. Dole used several maneuvers, in tandem with Senator Nancy Kassebaum of Kansas, the chief sponsor, to ensure that each one failed to stick. The one amendment that was certain to pass, one that would block funds to be used for "promoting homosexual service organizations," was thwarted by a subsequent amendment offered by Kassebaum that gutted its language.

So only months after AIDS groups had predicted the destruction of AIDS legislation as we knew it, Bob Dole supplanted Jesse Helms and ushered through a huge AIDS bill on the Senate floor. The gay press uncharacteristically gave credit to Dole for his accomplishment.

Two months later, in late August 1995, I received a call from Deb Price, a lesbian columnist for the *Detroit News*. She had pulled our Federal Election Commission report to see where our PAC money had been going, and was horrified that we had given money to Dole. I explained about his nondiscrimination policy, which included sexual orientation, and about his work on the Ryan White CARE Act. I also pointed out that Governor Pete Wilson of California, who was weeks away from announcing his own candidacy for president, had asked for our support and had received a $1,000 check from the LCR PAC. She thought that our support for Dole and also Pete Wilson was worth a story, and proceeded to call the Dole campaign.

I also called the campaign to give a heads-up on Price, but we were reassured that there was no problem there. In the months since I had given Dole that PAC check, things weren't looking good for the presumed front-runner. Phil Gramm had just pulled dead even with Dole in the Iowa straw poll, which sent the pundits reeling. Every major conservative voice in the Republican Party was criticizing Dole for being too moderate, for having a staff that was too open to centrist views. In particular, they were attacking his Senate chief of staff, Sheila Burke, who had opened the lines of communication with Log Cabin back in 1993 when Kevin Ivers and I met with her in the Capitol on the issue of gays in the military.

Moran called campaign manager Scott Reed, the former executive director of the Republican National Committee. The finance side of the campaign, made up largely of moderate Republicans, hadn't felt that it was worth telling Reed about Log Cabin's involvement with the campaign. Now it was going to be a story and Moran thought Reed should know about it. Undoubtedly with the Iowa straw poll on his mind, about which he'd just been interviewed by Richard Berke of *The New York Times*, spending the whole interview proclaiming how conservative Dole was going to be from now on, Reed went into a full-scale panic. Without contacting Dole, who was in New Hampshire, Reed released a written statement to Price claiming that the campaign would return the $1,000 check to the LCR, as the Dole campaign was in "100 percent disagreement with the agenda of Log Cabin Republicans."

When Deb Price called me and read the statement, it was very clear to me what was going on. I was shocked. How could they be so dumb? For better or worse, I felt I had no choice but to fire back. I called my friends on the finance committee, and was surprised when each of them tried to talk me into remaining silent. "Be a statesman. Don't say anything," said the woman who'd escorted me around Dole headquarters that day I first met with John Moran. "I promise we will work this out, and your steadfastness and statesmanship at this moment will be handsomely appreciated in the long run by the campaign."

All bets were off. They had declared war on the integrity of our organization. I didn't need to be affirmed; I was absolutely furious. In fact, only hours later I was on a plane to Cincinnati to open LCR's 1995 national convention, and would be bringing the news of the returned check to our most devoted activists, many of whom had joined our effort to support Dole's campaign with $1,000 checks of their own.

I soon learned that Dole had been totally out of the loop and had heard about Reed's action through a wire service piece in New Hampshire. I learned also that he was angry at his campaign manager, but was not going to second-guess his staff at a moment of crisis. To my disappointment, Dole defended Reed's actions when the press cornered him into commenting on the matter. Reed and campaign spokesman Nelson Warfield were telling reporters that our check had made it through their screening process by mistake—"a screw-up." Warfield even said we set up the campaign because we were "struggling for credibility." So I released all the personal correspondence with the campaign, showing the campaign's requests for funds and follow-up letters from our meetings. I was not going to let the lies stand.

Reed's attempted spin began to crumble, and the campaign was left looking craven and self-serving. Nearly every major English-language newspaper in the world, from *The New York Times* and the *Washington Post* to the *Atlanta Constitution* and the *Times* of London, ran an editorial or an opinion piece blasting Bob Dole and defending our integrity. Diverse radio personalities like Rush Limbaugh and Don

Imus used their shows to question Dole's move. Conservative columnist Robert Novak reported that on a trip to
Ohio he discovered that Dole's action had put the front-
runner in serious trouble with a wide range of party regu-
lars. In fact, not one column, editorial, or opinion piece
appeared in print in the mainstream media that defended
Dole's action. Gay staffers inside the Dole campaign, most
of whom had never done a thing for the gay community
previously, personally lobbied Dole to reverse his position.
Congressman Steve Gunderson, an openly gay Republican
from Wisconsin who had endorsed Dole early, wrote an
open letter challenging him in emotional, very personal
terms.

Around this time, General Colin Powell began testing
the waters for a run. People were comparing Powell's larger-
than-life image with Dole's patently unfair practice of returning checks to gay Republicans as if they were tainted.
The conservative *Washington Times* ran a political cartoon
depicting a campaign spokesman announcing that the
Dole campaign would "now be requiring a blood test with
each donation." The *Austin American-Statesman* showed a
cartoon of a spindly Dole pirouetting through a door and
leaping into the arms of a stunned elephant, saying "I'm
anti-gay!" The caption read: "Bob Dole comes out of the
conservative closet."

The unrelenting criticism in the press and from his own
supporters on the road—public words of reproach from
Governor George Pataki of New York, Governor Christie
Whitman of New Jersey, Senator Alfonse D'Amato, his national campaign co-chairman; private words of dismay from

former Republican National Committee co-chair Jeanie Austin in Florida and statewide campaign coordinators in the Midwest—was too much for Dole, particularly since it was an action with which he disagreed, and had he known of it in advance never would have allowed. He was asked about it almost a month after it happened on ABC-TV's *This Week with David Brinkley,* and when pressed by Sam Donaldson and Cokie Roberts, he seemed on the verge of irritably admitting that it was not his decision—but he still held back.

Finally, in an impromptu meeting in the Capitol in October 1995, Sabrina Eaton, a lesbian reporter for the *Plain Dealer* of Cleveland, asked Dole if he regretted the decision to return the Log Cabin check. The true story slipped out—he said he wasn't consulted, didn't approve of it, and wouldn't have done it if he'd known about it.

ABC-TV's *World News Tonight,* only hours later, reported Dole's turnabout. "It seems that $1,000 check from the Log Cabin Republicans has been everywhere and back again," Peter Jennings mused sarcastically. A smiling Senator Phil Gramm proudly told NBC that he'd never accept a Log Cabin check. And the *Washington Post,* in an editorial the next day, observed that our $1,000 check "must be the best-traveled cash in American politics."

Frank Rich of *The New York Times* summed it all up well in an op-ed piece titled "The Log Cabin Lesson":

> Bob Dole wishes that his less-than-excellent adventure with the gay Log Cabin Republicans would just go away, and no wonder. This farcical affair—during which Mr. Dole accepted a campaign contribution

from Log Cabin, then returned it, then this week said returning it had been a mistake—branded him not only as a flip-flopper but also as a hypocrite (why didn't he return any contributions to Time Warner?), a buck-passer (he blamed all the pratfalls on his staff), and a procrastinator (he let the embarrassing mess drag on for two months). It's hard to imagine how anyone could make a worse case for himself as a potential chief executive of anything, let alone the U.S.A.

But it would be a mistake to view this only as a story about Senator Dole. As Rich Tafel, executive director of Log Cabin, said to me in a postmortem interview this week, the story is "not really about homosexuality" either, but "about the soul of the party."

With only our integrity to stand on, gay Republicans had changed the course of gay politics and the presidential campaign, but not everyone in Washington understood that. In his book *The Choice*, Bob Woodward tells the story from Reed's perspective, blaming me for being a media hound, and pretending that his response to Price came days after the campaign accidentally deposited the check. I was disappointed that Woodward didn't call me to get the other side of the story.

With that exception, the incident showed the power of ideas and integrity. The media, and the press in particular, forced Bob Dole to apologize for something that was his staff's mistake. Months later, as the convention in San Diego loomed, Dole's coalitions organizer came to meet with us to seek our endorsement. I was still angry about the check, but put that behind me, as this was another unique, historic opportunity to make some headway for the gay community. This was politics, not therapy, and Bob Dole was going to control the convention in San Diego, where our goals needed to be met. I wasn't forgetting that reversing the course of 1992 was still our greatest objective.

We sought a commitment to maintain nondiscrimination policies for gay federal appointees, full funding for federal AIDS programs, a serious discussion with Log Cabin about employment nondiscrimination laws, a Republican National Convention free of gay bashing, the chance for an openly gay person to speak at the convention, an unwavering commitment that there be no anti-gay rhetoric or signs on the convention floor, and a public request for our endorsement. One by one, over time, each of our demands was met.

It began rolling when we arrived in San Diego. The ban on anti-gay speeches and signs was in place and was vigorously enforced. Along with a team of Log Cabin activists, I roamed the convention floor day and night, patrolling for violations. There were none. The tone was uplifting. In the same slot where Pat Buchanan brought the convention to a halt in 1992, Colin Powell stood up to say he was pro-choice and supported affirmative action, but that the party was "big enough and strong enough" to put aside differences on a few issues in order to unite for its common purpose of "restoring the American Dream." The tiny group of boos were drowned out by loud cheers from the Dole faithful. And going a step further, on the night that Dole took to the stage to accept the nomination of the Republican Party, a young gay activist from San Francisco named Stephen Fong, who was the president of the San Francisco Log Cabin Club, stood at the podium and gave a one-minute speech in support of Dole as a "main street American." His speech was prepared by the Dole campaign, and contained no references to his homosexuality, but for those of us in the audience the moment was something that would have been unimaginable four years earlier. That moment in Houston in 1992 so many in Log Cabin experienced as a nightmare had been transformed in 1996 into a small and symbolic but deeply important victory.

Two days later, Republican Party chairman Haley Barbour, not a particular friend of Log Cabin, approved the use of the RNC's press briefing room for Log Cabin Republicans to announce that it was moving ahead on endorsing the Dole-Kemp ticket, after the campaign announced, through spokeswoman Christina Martin, that it "welcomed the endorsement of the Log Cabin Republicans." I stood next to our small band of openly gay delegates and alternates and made the announcement about our endorsement proceeding, and was met with hostile, dismissive questions from gay reporters. Later in the campaign, in a meeting with Sheila Burke, the rest of our requests were publicly granted, including the pledge to maintain the nondiscrimination policies for federal workers and full funding for AIDS. Small steps forward, but crucially important in the long term, these breakthroughs in 1996 went unappreciated in the gay press. Gay reporters, mired in an unchanging worldview, continued to scratch their heads over why we even bothered.

A full three years from the day I attended the Dole fund-raiser that sparked all the controversy, I received a touching note from Nelson Warfield. Nelson had been the press person in the Dole campaign who had told the media that we lacked credibility and that our positions on the is- sues were too extreme for Dole to accept our support. His kind note to me admitted that mistakes were made: "I didn't feel good about how we handled it. And I don't now." He went on to explain that he was participating in an AIDS bike ride and asked for my support. "I hope the Ride will in some small way help me make right what was done two years ago."

I was very touched by this warm personal note, an un- usual surprise in Washington's rough-and-tumble environ- ment. In cynical Washington, it was a rare moment of integrity. Log Cabin gladly sponsored Nelson Warfield on his bike ride.

A Gay Political Strategy

The political challenge is clear. Gays need a political strategy in which they aren't taken for granted by Demo- crats or written off by Republicans. Today's gay movement must shift resources to the front lines, away from where it feels good, to where they are most needed. Politically, no single act would speed our advancement more quickly than for there to be a shift in political focus in the Republican Party—the front lines of the battle for gay equality. Chang- ing the Republican Party on gay issues should be the single most important goal of gay Democrats, Republicans, and Independents.

Additionally, a gay strategy for the next century needs to shift its effort away from a Washington-only focus to the grass roots. The front lines of the gay movement are at the state level, particularly in the South and Midwest. We need to support those who are courageous enough to accept the responsibility to organize outside urban areas and safe communities. We need to shift the focus away from federal legislation to local legislation. If the national gay organizations all pared themselves down to only a Washington coordinating staff with a few Hill lobbyists, and almost entirely dispersed their funds to the grassroots efforts, we would watch our movement leap forward toward our goals, creating a bubbling up of awareness and acceptance that Washington couldn't ignore.

A gay strategy for the next century needs to shift focus from increasing government involvement in our lives to removing current government barriers to gay equality. At the same time we are supporting federal employment bills, we should also support local efforts. Instead of focusing solely on new legislation, we should work to remove bad laws, such as the archaic sodomy laws and the latest barriers to serving in the military and having our relationships recognized. We need to support efforts to reduce the power of government over our lives. Instead of fearing the marketplace or the possibility of becoming victims of it, let us realize the opportunities that the free market offers us, particularly as we seek cures for AIDS and breast cancer.

We have to replace the victimization of identity politics with the empowerment of individual rights and responsibilities. Only we can ultimately take control of our destiny. We can't wait for Congress to pass a law before we come out at work. We can't pretend that AIDS spreads simply because government doesn't offer the requisite response. We need to take responsibility for our lives. But political strategy alone won't take us to the next phase of our movement; we need to articulate our moral vision.

Part 3: The Pursuit of Happiness

The Need for Gay Values in the Public Debate

"Mr. Falwell, I'm a Republican like you, and I'm also a Baptist like you. I'm a Christian, and my faith is very important to me. So, I'd just like to say that I wish you would stop pretending that you speak for all Christians when you say, 'as a Christian' it is wrong to be gay."

I was looking at a TV screen with the face of the Reverend Jerry Falwell on it in a Washington television studio, just before the Republican National Convention in 1992.

Our topic on CNN's *Larry King Live* that evening was whether a gay staffer should be allowed to work on the Bush reelection campaign, but I just got sick of his beating up on gay people in the name of Jesus.

I continued by pointing out to Falwell that he kept using selective passages from Scripture while ignoring others in his effort to bolster a political argument, much like Southern Baptists had used the passage from Ephesians— "Slaves, obey your earthly masters"—to justify slavery in America in the nineteenth century.

"Richard, I should have said a *Bible-believing* Christian," Falwell said with a grin.

"I believe in the Bible, too, Mr. Falwell," I responded impatiently.

"Do you take the Bible literally?" Falwell asked.

"No you don't," I countered. "Should slaves obey their masters?"

This had been the passage, taken literally, that split my church, the American Baptists, with the Southern Baptists more than one hundred years earlier. One thing that has always attracted me to the American Baptist Church was its leadership in the abolitionist movement.

"Do you take the Bible literally?" Falwell asked again, turning red-faced and angry.

"Should slaves obey their masters?" I asked again.

Falwell stumbled, trying to answer his own question by citing passages from Romans and Leviticus.

"Do you believe, Mr. Falwell—"

"I'm *against* slavery, and the Bible *condemns* slavery," Falwell said, stammering and pointing his finger.

"No, the Bible says, 'Slaves, obey your masters,' it says women should be silent in the church . . . ," I said, and Larry King went to a commercial break. Falwell was crimson with rage. During the commercial break King leaned over and said to me, "I like that Bible stuff you were just doing, that was good."

It is time for the gay movement to articulate in moral terms the values of our struggle for our place in the American family. As we get beyond the rejection reaction, beyond hurt feelings that have led us to a desperate need to be liked, beyond the pretense that we must simply be left alone, we must begin to articulate our guiding values.

What made the debate with Falwell different is that I refused to yield the moral high ground to him. I refused to meet his Christian values argument with a simple call for tolerance. The danger of speaking only about tolerance is that while Americans treasure it as a principle, they won't move beyond tolerance to true acceptance until gays begin making the moral argument.

As the Falwell debate dramatizes, the debate over homosexuality leads to one basic question: Are gay people inherently immoral? It is really nothing less than two very different views of God, two different views of right and wrong. This is a debate we simply cannot engage in through a call for the separation of church and state alone. Even in secular America, an overwhelming number of people believe in God, and the religious right has appealed to believers and nonbelievers alike by saying that *God* says homosexuals are sinful.

Frank Kameny, one of the earliest leaders of the gay

movement, though not a religious person, himself addressed this need in his early motto, "Gay is good!" We must make it clear that to be gay isn't immoral, it just is what it is. It isn't a lifestyle choice, it is a reality of life. It is a movement based on people who love people of the same gender. The gay life is not inherently good or evil, neither moral nor immoral, but to lie about who you are and to discriminate against people because they are different, that *is* immoral, and the gay movement needs to articulate that point.

The need for gay values goes well beyond the public debate. The greater challenge will be for gays to recognize our need for values and spirituality to guide our daily lives.

Confusing Mores and Morals

As a gay Christian, the saddest reality for me has been that the leading opposition to the equal treatment of gays in our society comes from people like Jerry Falwell, who abuse gays in the name of Jesus. Going head-to-head with the Jerry Falwells of this world, I can completely understand why many gays fear any talk of faith, Christianity, religion, and spirituality.

Although I was raised in a Baptist Church, my familial faith is in a small Protestant denomination, called Swedenborgian. This church is most famous for its mystical insights and teachings about eternal life. One key teaching is that all faith is good.

In fact, Swedenborg, during one of his glimpses into heaven, describes the shocking paradox that leaders of the religious establishment are living in a hell of their own creation, while people of all faiths and good people of no faith are making their way through the World of Spirits to heaven. This ecumenicalism has always been a part of my belief, and was why I was so attracted to the ecumenical work at Harvard's Memorial Church.

In my own experience I've met wonderful people of faith, awful people of faith, and incredible people with no religious tradition at all. So I tread humbly in espousing my Christian faith—the spiritual impetus for all of my work. Jesus' teachings of the call to love, the need for forgiveness, the importance of patience, the importance of humility, being nonjudgmental, the lessons of suffering, the promise of eternal life, and compassion for the outcasts, I believe, still offer valuable lessons for today's gay community. The fundamental lesson of Jesus is the fundamental lesson of most all spiritual movements: "To love your neighbor, as you love yourself." For the gay community, loving a neighbor who calls you sick and perverted is tough. And for a community that still internalizes the hatred it's experienced for being gay, loving oneself may be harder yet.

It is a sad irony that much of the meanness in our world is perpetrated in the name of God. Too often throughout history, the Christian Church has become co-opted by earthly powers losing sight of the radically compassionate message of Jesus. The Church too often confuses mores (time-based cultural norms) with morals (spiritually based, eternal, universal values). When the Church becomes wedded with the earthly power of its day, it comes to accept the social norms, and convinces itself that these temporal customs have spiritual value that the Church must uphold. For this reason, the Church has a sad tradition of being on the wrong side of most of the great moral debates of history.

During the Holocaust, only a handful of Christians in Germany opposed the Third Reich. It is no accident that my cousin Dietrich Bonhoeffer is also one of my role models for my work in Log Cabin. When he applied his faith against the Third Reich, it led him to help Jews escape, to preach against the state, and eventually brought him into the plot to assassinate Hitler. The saddest time for modern Christianity was when the churches of Germany and Italy worked with their Fascist governments. If Christians couldn't speak out in the face of the mass murder of Jews, it raises the hard question whether God is still active in this world through the Church. The fact that Bonhoeffer and a few others stood against Hitler in the name of Jesus, in my opinion, did nothing less than redeem the Christian faith from its worst moment in modern history.

When we watch courageous people in difficult situations like Nazi Germany, we ask ourselves, what would we do? I take great pride in the fact that Bonhoeffer's grandmother, Julie Tafel Bonhoeffer, the morning after Kristallnacht, purposefully marched into Jewish stores to make purchases. This, despite the fact that she was ninety years old and SA brownshirts stood in front of every Jewish store.

At his grandmother's funeral, Bonhoeffer offered this reflection on her Christian faith: "Thus her last years were clouded by the great grief she endured over the fate of the Jews among our people, a fate she bore and suffered in sympathy with them. She was the product of another time, of another spiritual world—and that world does not go down with her to the grave." Each generation is faced with a threat to human dignity, and far too often the Church is on the wrong side of the debate. Yet the Church's salvation is that the opposition to evil usually comes through faith in the prophetic voices of people like my cousin.

The treatment of Jews in Europe and blacks in America are two recent historical examples of the Church defending mores, not morals. For centuries, the Church mimicked societal injunctions against women, despite the fact that Jesus was radically supportive of women. Society kept women in subservient roles, and the Church reinforced those mores. The industrial society gave women more freedoms, and years later the Church slowly mimicked those advances. Today, the information age offers women radically more freedom, and the Church, still acting on old mores, is slowly catching up. The Church missed its opportunity to lead on the issue of the dignity of women. Even today, the pope defends not having women priests based on there being no record of them at the Last Supper, forgetting entirely that women were the first to find the empty tomb—in a sense, they were the first Christians.

But no one should wait for the Church to apologize in this lifetime, because the Church traditionally has been slow to admit its mistakes. The Roman Catholic Church took five hundred years to apologize to Galileo for nearly executing him for his belief that the Earth rotated around the Sun. The Church took fifty years to apologize for working in collusion with Nazi Germany and Fascist Italy. The

Southern Baptists took one hundred years to apologize for their advocacy of the slavery of African-Americans. Someday the Church will seek repentance for the evil perpetrated today against gays and lesbians.

The arrogance of today's religious leaders who claim they alone speak for those who care about family is galling. But their confusion between mores and morals in defining a true Christian family is nothing new. The Christian leaders of the early 1800s warned of dangers to the "modern family." The family that Church leaders criticized then, the so-called nuclear family, is the same family that Church leaders defend now. In a world with expanding choices and disorder, the religious right nurtures the comfort of a nostalgic past.

Straight, white, wealthy men who were "masters of the universe" in an earlier age naturally view the past with great nostalgia. In the 1950s, their world was clear. People knew their place in society. While there might have been widespread dissatisfaction with the altogether repressive conditions in which many people lived, there was no widespread sense of displacement. This kind of nostalgia is assessed by author Bruce Bawer in his book *Stealing Jesus*, in which he discusses James Dobson and his multimillion-dollar religious right organization, Focus on the Family: "His is the voice of every middle-class white heterosexual male who feels that everything was just fine in the old days, when blacks didn't dare cry out against their oppression, gays huddled voicelessly in the closet, and women were meek, pliant housewives."

To today's religious leader who plays on fears rather

than hopes, homosexuality is the perfect "sin." For some who are heterosexual, it is a "sin" they never need to worry about committing, which allows them to condemn it with great authority. The sin of homosexuality allows William Bennett to lecture President Clinton for attending a gay black-tie dinner and for not confronting gays for "leading lives that bring an early death." Yet Bennett sits there, clearly very overweight and an avowed smoker, and no leader of the religious right will challenge the sin of obesity or of tobacco abuse, as they hit too close to home. Lifestyles like Mr. Bennett's lead to more deaths through heart disease than any other killer, but too many fundamentalists engage in such lifestyles for them to become the fodder of direct mail campaigns.

People generally fear what is different. Homosexual behavior is different and difficult for straight people to imagine, making it easy to caricature and lie about. Lurid exaggerations and lies about homosexuality scare people enough for them to write a check and send it to the religious right group of the moment. There's no doubt in my mind that the bulk of gay bashing by right-wing groups in America today is motivated by fund-raising demands. With the turn of the century coming, listen for the rantings of these self-proclaimed prophets of doom to hit a fever pitch, such as Pat Robertson's very public and solemn admonition in 1998 that because the city of Orlando flew rainbow flags on its streets, it was inviting "hurricanes, terrorist bombs, earthquakes, and maybe even a meteor" to strike and destroy it.

For others who secretly know they are gay, yet live in

fear of having to confront the reality, their leadership in opposition is proof that they aren't gay. In college, while I fought the reality of being gay, I made sure to date attractive women to assuage doubts. I lobbied a very anti-gay Massachusetts state senator once about gay rights. As he replied to my comments, he grew louder and more agitated. He told me about a friend he knew who had homosexual leanings, but got married and had children and kept those evil feelings at bay. By the time he finished speaking, he was screaming at me. It was clear that his friend was himself and his yelling was an effort to be convincing. It is no accident that many opponents of gay rights themselves project stereotypical homosexual behavior.

Understanding the Religious Right

In June 1997, I attended a conference of socially conservative scholars entitled "Homosexuality and American Society" at Georgetown University. It brought together, possibly for the first time, Orthodox Jews, fundamentalist Protestants, and Roman Catholics in a meeting intended to show the unity of moral people of faith in opposition to homosexuality. By the conference's end, the attendees all learned just how different their own respective "truths" on homosexuality really were—all that they had in common was a willingness to play on their followers' fears.

When I entered the conference, my old sparring partner, Tony Falzarano of Transformation Ex-Gay Ministries, waved to me from the front of the room, where he was about to give a presentation. Tony and I had had lunch a few times and we'd argued frequently on radio talk shows. On one program, Tony paid me the compliment of declaring, "I think Rich is a closet Christian. I believe he is very close to being a true Christian." To which I responded, "One of us is in the closet, and it isn't me."

Lunches with Tony were always a treat. He had been a hustler in the 1970s, and at one time a call boy of the despicable Roy Cohn, former counsel to Senator Joseph McCarthy. It was fascinating to hear him tell stories about Roy buying him this or that. The stories always concluded with him defending the closeted and anti-gay Roy Cohn as a great man, and then, snap, like a light switch going off, Tony would proclaim his love for Jesus and his new life in Christ. By understanding his troubled background, I find it easier to forgive the sometimes hateful language he uses. Sadly, Tony has been paid and used as a poster boy for the religious right. He once bragged to me, "And Pat Robertson has written a personal check to me!"

His newfound self-righteousness makes it almost impossible for him to work in any coalition. Tony spoke about his life as an out homosexual, predicting that in a few years the Ex-Gay Ministries would hold mass meetings in football stadiums, much like the Promise Keepers. A questioner asked Tony how he planned to fill stadiums with "ex-gays" if the gay movement was so powerful. Tony paused for a minute. He was okay when his comments were written, but when he answered questions, he was on less sure footing and often displayed a knack for being off message. He responded, "Well, I'll be honest with you, I believe we are in the end times. I think many people will be coming to Christ to obtain salvation because we are in the end times." By "the end times," he was referring to the end of the world as foretold in the New Testament's Book of Revelation.

I happened to be sitting behind two Orthodox Jews with payess, beards, and yarmulkes. They glared at each other with great anxiety, one stroking his beard and the other biting his nails as they whispered back and forth. The Orthodox speaker early that day had stunned his evangelical audience when he stated that in his understanding of the Torah homosexuality was a sin, but not as much a sin as gossip. Tony also hadn't exactly kept to the ecumenical script for the conference. The limits of Judeo-Christian coalition in opposition to homosexuality were showing.

The Catholic view of the homosexual crisis was presented by Patrick Fagan, a Fitzgerald Fellow at the Heritage Institute. Fagan traced the demise of the American family back to 1930, when the Anglican Church made allowances for birth control. As he explained it, this decision detached sex from its proper foundational purpose—procreation. "The sex act," he claimed, "is ordained unto the child." Fagan made the case that the highest human act was to participate in creation with God. Birth control, masturbation, and abortion are examples of mankind telling God that they refused to join Him in humanity's highest calling. He professed not a worldview from the words of Jesus, but one that was based on the agrarian culture of long ago. Fagan described homosexuality as one of many "cultures of death" that were a natural outgrowth of a society inverted selfishly upon itself—a culture that had forgotten the fundamental purpose of sex.

In an interesting twist, though, unlike the evangelical Protestants in attendance, Fagan held to the Roman Catholic perspective that homosexuality is inborn behavior, and not a choice. This was in direct opposition to Tony's self-assured "cured" presentation at the conference. This fissure widened when a few months later the U.S. Conference of Catholic Bishops issued a pastoral letter, calling homosexual behavior a sin, but stating that since homosexuality itself was not a choice, it therefore was not a sin—only acting on it was. The letter went on to urge parents to accept their gay and lesbian children, and parishes to open their doors to gay Catholics and fearlessly love them.

The diversity of views among these people of God attending the conference appeared to be causing more confusion than clarity. Each of these self-righteous people of faith got up to tell how God hated the sin of homosexuality based on very clear biblical, talmudic, or natural law doctrines, and yet even among these traditionalists there were chasms of disagreement. Nonetheless, the confusion displayed at the conference hasn't caused these leaders to pause and question their own interpretation of God's word or of homosexuality. Each marches forward, without an ounce of humility, in his or her battle against the gay person.

Sitting for so long among such people it is good to maintain a sense of humor. Robert Knight of the Family Research Council went on a tirade against Disney and its products for the corporation's gay-friendly policies. Andrew Sullivan, who was sitting next to me, pointed to the woman on my other side, who was wearing a Mickey Mouse wrist-watch. I couldn't resist, and at the break I asked her for the time. She briefly flashed her watch, and I gave a very disapproving look. In their bizarre confusion of mores and morals, even Mickey Mouse could become a symbol of the devil.

In my opinion, there is no greater sin that the churches are committing during this time in history than turning gay people away from a relationship with God. Jesus didn't mince words when he said, "If any of you put a stumbling block before one of these little ones who believe in me, it would be better for you if a great millstone were fastened around your neck and you were drowned in the depth of the sea" (Matthew 18:6).

One recent funny experience gives me hope that the tide is slowly turning against the power of the religious right. As I waited one afternoon for the shuttle from the Washington Hilton to Dulles Airport, on my way to California, I realized that, once again, I hadn't really given myself enough time to catch my flight. I decided to bite the bullet and take a cab, expensive though it would be. Always the fiscal conservative, I offered to my fellow travelers waiting for the bus the chance to share a ride and split the costs.

An older woman, also worried about making her flight, decided to join me. As we sat in the back seat, I pulled my baseball cap over my eyes, hoping to get some sleep. She wanted to chat, however, and insisted on playing Twenty Questions the entire way out. I answered with monosyllabic replies, but she kept on. She seemed most interested in what type of work I do, which is always a conversation piece. I did not want to engage, just sleep.

"You're in politics aren't you?" she asked. "Yep," I responded. "You're involved in Republican Party politics, aren't you?" "Yep." "You're involved with social issues in the Republican Party," she continued, her voice becoming more agitated. "Yes, I am," I said. "Were you on C-SPAN lately?" she asked. "Yes, I was."

"Well, I know who you are!" she said, pointing her finger in the air. "And, let me say this to you, young man. I find your work repugnant. I'm a Republican. And I think it is awful what you've done in the Republican Party and the country. You, and your agenda, you've brought nothing but divisiveness to the Republican Party. Your efforts will fail, good people will stand up and you will fail.

"I know who you are," she said again to me as I just looked out the window, asking God why in the world I got stuck in this cab with this woman. "You're Ralph Reed!"

In my work, you have to treasure these rare comical moments. The two of us went on to have a positive conversation about the importance of treating gays fairly. I believe the tide is turning against the religious right's campaign of fear.

Limits of Therapeutic Relativism

Everyone needs values, a code of what is important to guide their lives, and gays and lesbians are no exception. As I've shown, the Church has done a good job of chasing gays away from God and the guidance of the Judeo-Christian teachings. As gays were being attacked by churches and kicked out of their homes in the name of family values, a new value system was gaining in popularity throughout the country—a nonjudgmental, therapeutic human potential movement. This movement posited no right or wrong, but called on its disciples to take care of themselves and be honest with themselves—to do what was right for themselves. Most every gay person I know has benefited in some way from therapy of one kind or another. Yet though it has great strengths, the therapeutic human potential movement also has its limitations. In offering no right or wrong, no good or evil, no moral or immoral, it leads to a relativism.

I wrote an op-ed article for the *San Francisco Chronicle* that criticized Tony Valenzuela, a spokesman for Sex Panic, a liberationist group. Tony implied in a speech I attended that he had no obligation to not infect others with the HIV virus. "Let's say it loud and clear," I stated, "it is immoral to knowingly infect another person with a deadly disease." This might sound obvious in the extreme, but within the gay community language of morality is so feared that those who defended the activist's comments claimed that it wasn't the HIV-infected person's job to protect the person he was with. If the receptive partner allows himself to get infected, well, that's his own fault, they reasoned. It was the responsibility of each person to look after himself. "What is the meaning of the gay community?" I asked. After years of being beaten up by moralizers, our community had rebelled against the very concept of right and wrong, even about potentially infecting another person with a deadly disease.

In 1994, the International Lesbian and Gay Association (ILGA) was about to lose its charter at the United Nations because Senator Jesse Helms discovered that one of the association's member groups was the North American Man-Boy Love Association (NAMBLA), a group that promotes pedophilia, couching its arguments in terms of liberationist self-determination. During this controversy, one of its spokesmen, on CNN's *Larry King Live,* defended sex between men and boys as young as eight years old.

In this debate, the gay community's moral relativism model was at a loss. The liberationists stressed self-determination, which would include the rights of adults to have sex with eight-year-old children. Yet others, particularly gay women, began to enunciate their personal disgust about the exploitation of kids. The assimilationists, on the other hand, long embarrassed by the charges of pedophilia, saw a public relations debacle but responded with no moral outrage, confused because they didn't want to cede any ground to Jesse Helms.

Underlying the awkward silence on the NAMBLA controversy in the gay community is a deeply held, unspoken belief, the feeling that because we ourselves as gays are not good, and we have no moral leg upon which we can stand, we cannot condemn anyone else's sexual choices. In other words, we who stand in our own glass house can't throw stones. And if we have no moral authority in our cause, just tolerance, then what possible right or criteria do we have to exclude NAMBLA? If gays don't believe themselves moral, but simply tolerated, then any action taken by anyone must be tolerated as well, even sex with eight-year-old children.

I wrote a controversial op-ed piece at the time, drawing on the time-honored moral belief that children are children and they need to be protected against those who would, under the guise of self-determination, exploit them. I was making a distinction between gay adult behavior as moral and exploitive sex with young kids as immoral. Eventually other national gay groups opposed NAMBLA, but with great difficulty because they had no criteria by which to say that what NAMBLA was doing was wrong. My op-ed piece led one NAMBLA supporter to write me and say, "I'd rather tolerate pedophiles than gay Republicans."

The human potential movement is also very pragmatic. If something works, then it's okay. This philosophy permeates much of our society, and it's especially prevalent in the gay community. The gay leaders who support my work usually do so only in terms of pragmatism. "Well, thank God someone can lobby Republicans on key issues that I care about," they say. They also see my ordination and faith as pragmatically valuable. "Rich is great when he debates the religious right, because he knows the Bible and throws it right back at them." As a person engaged in the pragmatic political debate every day, I do understand the importance of it, but I refuse to justify my work solely on the limited basis of pragmatism while forgetting the power of our values and our morality.

Most of the gay movement and much of the media have convinced themselves that American politics is simply a mechanical battle of fund-raising strength and turning out voting blocs for candidates, forgetting the power of principles and values and transforming ideas. Ultimately, our small community is going to win this national debate on the moral level, not the pragmatic one. We will never have enough of our own money or votes to win our cause. Time after time gay leaders trumpet or bemoan their budgets and organizational strength, but numbers alone won't win the day. We must engage in and win the debate through the power of our values and the power that sharing those values has to transform society.

In the civic debate we must articulate the values that guide us; for example, I'm a Republican because I believe less government and free markets best address the human condition of original sin—they harness selfishness and prevent any one person from being too powerful. These political beliefs alone, without a belief in the transforming power of God and justice, would make me cynical and politics little more than a game, a perpetual power struggle.

Yet I'm an idealist, though the changes I seek won't be brought about through any government or party, but through the transformation of the hearts of individuals and then the larger society. The pursuit of happiness for me is both the personal right of individuals to achieve their own success and the challenge for the society to practice justice for everyone. The moral debate takes us beyond the practical debate. We must always articulate our ideals and vision in the public debate.

We could also do a better job of understanding the pragmatic concerns of politicians and attempting to determine whether they are good people. I've seen situations in which a candidate is giving a speech to a gay audience and uses a politically incorrect term, such as "sexual preference" instead of "orientation," and faces the wrath of the audience, which tells him he didn't get the words right. The moral debate requires that we take a look into people's hearts and motives, not simply police the words they use. And it requires us to examine those who use the right words to understand what values motivate them.

Gay leaders have made great progress by stressing pragmatic reasons for supporting gay rights—which is absolutely necessary—but typically haven't stressed the underlying moral arguments enough. During the debate about gays in the military, the gay community was stunned that the president never made a public address to defend his position. I believe the reason is that the issue was never presented to him in moral terms, so he never really understood the moral implications of forcing people to lie so they can die for their country.

The evolution of the issue was totally pragmatic. Gay Democrats gave candidate Clinton a list of issues of importance. He chose the military issue, probably because he thought it was the safest. There was no consensus on the issue of gays in the military in the gay community, particularly the liberal gay community. Clinton liked it, his gay supporters had an issue they could flash to the gay community, and that's basically how the issue was chosen. The only ones who really seemed to understand the moral importance of serving honestly were the soldiers who, on the president's word, came out. (They were all eventually discharged.)

Gay leaders who addressed the issue often spoke in pragmatic terms, thus playing into the hands of the opposition, which declared that the military had become the laboratory for a liberal experiment.

In every debate in which the gay political leadership engages, it must stress the morality of the cause. At the end of the day, we will win our battle because we have the moral high ground, not because we raised enough money or got enough people to vote. Those pragmatic concerns will follow only after we make our case on moral grounds.

Moral Transformation in the Civic Debate

My Washington friends tend to think that all of my talk about moral transformation in the civic debate makes me naive, and I counter that our cynical age has lost track of the power of transforming ideas and ideals. Though gay leaders always look to the work of *Doctor* Martin Luther King Jr. in the civil rights movement as a role model, they have yet to enunciate the Christian and Gandhian spiritual values of the *Reverend* Martin Luther King Jr. Today's activists behave as though King simply used clever political strategies, such as boycotts and direct action, while completely forgetting the Christian faith that defined every step of his mission.

I know I am a great paradox or even an oxymoron for many. I am a Republican based on certain long-standing American civic principles, yet have little respect for those who currently define my party. You might say I am Republican in spite of the party. In the same way, I am a devout Christian, in spite of those who currently define the Church. And while my civic principles guide me in the political arena, the public square of politics is the arena for our country's great moral debates. My Christian faith transcends the temporal concerns of which piece of legislation or candidate I support. Gays cannot allow their fear of the messenger to stop them from considering the importance of spiritual values in guiding our debate and our daily lives.

My Christian faith is, as Bonhoeffer calls it, an active faith. It is not spun from the ivory tower of a theological school, but based on my experiences on the front lines of one of America's meanest culture wars. During one of my "sadomasochistic" appearances on the far right's National Empowerment Television cable channel, I had the opportunity to debate Robert Knight of the Family Research Council. Robert, after politely chatting with me before the program in the green room, launched into a personal war of annihilation once we were on the air, arguing that he loved gay people and wanted them to stop destroying themselves in the gay lifestyle. The lifestyle he described was one in which men ingest feces and recruit young schoolchildren for sex, and in which the average life expectancy for those without AIDS is forty-two. Robert didn't just disagree with me, he was vicious, and by any measure un-Christ-like, though he claimed to speak on behalf of Christian values.

I did all I could to maintain my composure, responding that it appeared Robert knew much more about this bizarre lifestyle than I or any gay person I'd ever met. I also refused to let him speak as though he alone spoke for people of faith, and we engaged in some Bible debates. I explained that being a Christian did give my life a sense of right and wrong, but also required a confession of my own sin, which made me humble in my approach to others. Friends always ask me why I bother going on such programs, as clearly Robert Knight isn't interested in the truth of my life, and the audiences are generally hostile.

In such an environment, I can only hope to be a witness, and invariably something transforming takes place. Following our debate, our host went to phone-in questions from the viewing audience. NET was a cable channel that you subscribed to, so I knew that the calls were going to be one-sided—against me. The first caller described me as disgusting and sick. Another caller insisted I wasn't a real Republican. The third caller was furious about my calling myself a Christian. I began to feel like a human punching bag—slam, bam, boom.

But I'll never forget the next caller, one from North Carolina. All I could think was that he was calling from the home of Jesse Helms. He began speaking with a very thick Southern accent—now I knew I was in trouble. He began, "Mr. Knight, I don't support homosexuality. But I've watched how you've tried to destroy that young man next to you for the past half hour. And I've heard him humbly respond to your attack, and I've heard him say that he's a confessed Christian right here on the air. And your attacks on him are profoundly unchristian. Well, if he's a Christian, then he, like the rest of us, is washed in the blood of Jesus. And if he's washed in the blood of Jesus and proclaims his faith humbly, then he'll receive salvation. As for you, Mr. Knight, you don't come off as a Christian at all. And let me just say this, I expect to see that young man in heaven someday. Thank you."

★

The blessing of being gay is that our own experience with suffering can lead us to new levels of compassion. Those of us who are from the reformed Protestant tradition don't have a very developed theology of suffering. In fact, I think I've stayed away from it as much as possible. But Jesus teaches again and again the power that comes through suffering.

Gays and lesbians have suffered much. One third of all young gays have attempted suicide, and most, including myself, have at one time seriously thought about it. That suffering, which comes from being rejected by parents, family, school, church, and friends, allows us the choice to either become bitter victims or have a deeper sense of empathy for people under attack, people who are different. If gays and lesbians translate that lesson of suffering into a new sense of compassion and empathy, we could lead the greater society, which itself struggles with divisions.

The strangest experience I had with the power of empathy came during my debate at Georgetown University with Martin Mawyer of the Christian Action Network on the topic of gay marriage. His point was that marriage and the family were biblical institutions created for the purpose of procreation. I then asked him which biblical family he meant, and I began reading from the first chapter of the first book of Kings, which states that King Solomon had six hundred wives and three hundred concubines. Mawyer just looked baffled, as though I were reading from some strange text. What I've found most striking in my numerous debates with "religious leaders" is their pick-and-choose use of Scripture.

"But Jesus was about traditional family values," Martin countered. Typically, when fundamentalist debaters find something that appears contradictory in the Old Testament (even though they supposedly take every word literally), they claim that the biblical model was based solely on the teachings of Jesus and the letters of Paul.

But there's no New Testament basis for the Ozzie and Harriet world of the American fundamentalists either. In fact, in the story of young Jesus, He is a child of twelve leaving His parents to teach in the temple. After they find Him, Jesus chastises them, saying incredulously, "Did you not know that I must be about My Father's business?" Jesus said that He didn't come to bring peace, but a sword, to pit family members against one another. Equally unsupportive of the traditional family is Jesus' response to a question about Mary, His mother, and His brothers who wish to see him. Jesus responds by asking rhetorically, "Who is My mother and who are My brothers? . . . For whoever does the will of My Father in heaven is My brother and sister and mother." Jesus himself is no role model for the nuclear family, He remains single until his death—no wife, no kids.

I continued by asking Martin about Pat Buchanan's childless marriage, and whether God blessed that union. Or should we bar the elderly from marrying? Mawyer was losing ground in the debate. It was also clear that the student audience was hostile to him. When it came time for questions, the students took a flippant, dismissive tone toward him. After he floundered in his answers, the students began a verbal pile-on. The tone of the questioners became more snide; they often left the mike with a snicker or a personal put-down of Mawyer.

I glanced over at him, and could see that he was losing it. He was sweating profusely and his answers often bore no connection to the question. The political debating instincts in me smelled blood. The comment of a friend who is a campaign operative ran through my mind: "When you get your opponent down, that's when you step on his neck!"

But something very strange happened. In spite of myself, my Christian faith kicked in. I felt an incredible compassion for Mawyer. A student was arguing the illogic of Martin's comments, and ended his own comments with something about Martin being "stupid." It was my turn to respond, to complete the pile-on.

"Of course I disagree with Martin," I began, "but I do feel he is arguing from his heart. I don't think it is fair to call him names or imply that he's stupid. Martin and I have debated in numerous arenas, and he's always argued ideas, never once getting personal with me. So, I'd ask everyone to try to listen to what he's trying to say, and hold back on any mean, personal comments."

I looked out at the audience and saw most students had a sense of bewilderment on their faces. I was like a boxer, holding up his wobbling opponent. I could tell that they didn't get it. I wasn't sure I got it either. But Martin got it. "Well, let me just say," he began in his thick Southern accent, "that I have nothing but the highest respect for Rich. I appreciate his last comments. And I can tell you, if the gay community were all like Rich, we wouldn't be having a culture war in this country."

I will always remember this moment as one of the most bizarre in my political life. After the debate, Martin practically gave me a hug. The students seemed perplexed and put off by my request that we stop the name-calling. One student in the audience said to me as we walked out, "You blew it. You had him in the scope, and you just couldn't pull the trigger." In some strange way I felt it was a transforming evening of politics, if not for the audience, then, at least, for Martin and me. The ability to forgive and defend Martin transcended the points I could make in the moment and reminded me that I was a person of faith engaged in the political arena, not a politico using the rhetoric of faith.

Learning to love and forgive your enemy is the most challenging and powerful and ultimately successful reaction we gays can have to the rejection we experience. I think the hardest and most important principle for any human being, and I put myself at the top of the list, is to offer forgiveness. In the end, I believe this is the only true antidote to the hatred of the religious right.

Our anger has allowed us to become in so many ways as intolerant and angry as the religious right that we so much define ourselves in opposition to. Only forgiveness, an attempt to understand the opposition, will break the vicious cycle. Those who return hate for hate are eventually consumed by it.

Moral Transformation in Politics

The battle for equality will require patience too. I understand the impatience of gays toward the attitudes of straights, but patience and understanding can make a difference. Following a long day of lobbying a Republican Senate candidate about gay issues, I was feeling very good about the progress we made. He had asked honest questions and we even talked about our faith. We were getting toward the end of the meeting, when he mentioned he had one other question. "You don't want gays to be Boy Scout leaders, do you? I mean, aren't gays more likely to hit on the kids?"

"Patience," I said to myself as I took a deep breath and told the candidate of my years of working with kids. It wasn't easy, but it proved to be worthwhile. He turned out to become one of the most gay-supportive candidates in the country that year; he won his race, and serves in the U.S. Senate today.

The last time I took a member of another gay organization on a Republican lobbying visit, the topic was employment. The Republican staffer cavalierly dismissed with a smile the need for gays to be protected, saying, "Come on, gays have much more money than straights. Jeez, you practically run Hollywood. Look at [David] Geffen and [Barry] Diller."

Before I could patiently and politely respond, the other group's lobbyist shouted back, "That's easy for you to say, but not for Cheryl Sommerville" (a lesbian who had been fired from the Cracker Barrel restaurant chain, but the staffer had no idea who she was). The other lobbyist almost started to cry as she began yelling at the staffer. He turned to me and said, "Gee, I'm sorry. I'm sorry if I hurt your feelings," as he quickly ended the meeting. We must get beyond hurt feelings, develop a sense of ourselves, and patiently and compassionately educate those who simply don't understand.

A leading centrist Republican from Pennsylvania, whom I visited during the heat of the gays in the military issue, had been dubbed a "homophobe" by the Campaign for Military Service for his vote on the issue. "They've burned their bridges with me," he told me. "Listen, it has taken many of you who are gay a long time to come to a personal understanding of what that means. Won't you please have the patience to help those of us who are not gay to come to a better understanding on this too? Calling us names is not going to help your cause. I'm trying to get a handle on this."

Today, he has become a member of the senior House Republican leadership, and is one of the most supportive members on the Hill on the inclusion of all Americans. He was asking for patience as he worked from opposition through tolerance to support. But what if the only gay group he encountered was one that demonized him?

★

We can model moral integrity in our political work too. Our integrity is our most powerful weapon. When we give our word on Capitol Hill or anywhere, let us live by what we say.

When gay groups claim to be bipartisan, yet continue to work a one-party strategy, we may fool those on the Hill, but we'll only do it once. After that, important doors are shut.

In 1994, when members of the Log Cabin Republicans from a Midwestern state met in the House cloakroom with a Republican representative from that state, she was fairly new to Congress. She was polite but cool, and so were our members. Toward the end of our meeting, one of our board members, John Kost, asked her for a simple favor: "When you hear gay bashing in the Republican conference, would you tell your fellow members to stop?" John is very low-key, and I was surprised that he asked so directly. But I was more surprised by her response: "I don't know that I can do that." I was stunned that she wouldn't do more. John replied, "That's all we can ask."

Over the next few years, the group continued to meet with her. Following one meeting about AIDS funding, one member of the group told of his personal battle with the disease. As the meeting closed, she teared up and hugged him. She rapidly grew in stature in the GOP conference and her courage to stand up for gays has grown as well. At their most recent meeting, when one member told her that Log Cabin had never had a formal meeting with the party leadership, she replied, "Indefensible! I'll walk you over personally to make sure you get a meeting."

Again and again, I witness the power of ideas and faith. I listen endlessly to the debate over campaign finance reform. The media and most people have bought into the concept that money alone can buy politicians. And through my work I know that simply isn't true. Time after time, I watch Republican politicians reach out to gay people be-cause they know in their heart it is the right thing to do. In discussing our position with them, I invariably make the pragmatic case for treating gays fairly, but I also make the moral case. And that's the one that usually wins the day. If our movement is ever to extend beyond the urban centers where there are large populations of gays, we must make the moral argument.

When Mayor Rudolph Giuliani introduced a wide-ranging domestic partnership bill in the New York City Council, the press and pundits were aghast. Didn't he know that this would kill his political chances for national office? What was he thinking? And Tom Duane, a gay liberationist member of the City Council, showed his true colors too, when he said it was the best we can expect from a Republi-can. What few could believe is, as I told *The New York Times*, that he might have done it just because he had become convinced it was the right thing to do. I made the point that the moral approach could actually have pragmatic benefits for a cynical generation.

When the issue of domestic partnerships came up while I worked for Governor Weld in Massachusetts, the ad-vice from his staff was not to support the policy. When the governor finished his meeting, he announced to his gay supporters that he had some good news and some bad news. The bad news was that it was the most unpopular is-sue ever to come before his staff. The vote had been eight against and one for. The good news was that he was the one—the policy was enacted. He valued what was right over any political calculation and his popularity rose.

I remember a member of Weld's staff, a closeted gay Republican who confronted me on this issue days later. "Great job on domestic partners, Rich," he snarled sarcastically. "You've just ruined any chance that Bill would be president. Way to go." To which I responded, "Do you think being president is the most important thing Weld can do? He did the right thing, which will live on long after he is out of politics." I was reminded of the verse "For what will it profit a man if he gains the whole world, and loses his own soul?"

Most of the Republicans that Log Cabin members have worked with have become more supportive on gay issues. Puzzled gay leaders ask, "How did you get him on our side? What's his real agenda?" Others wonder how we bullied that Republican into supporting us. I respond: "We spoke with him and listened to him and treated his ideas with respect, and patiently answered his questions. We built on common ground, we challenged him morally, and we offered pragmatic benefits." And what has most impressed me, even in deepest, darkest Washington, D.C., is the desire of so many people to try to do what is right when it is presented in moral terms. I remember thanking Republican senator John McCain of Arizona for his support of Jim Kolbe following Kolbe's coming out as a gay man. He responded, "What choice did I have? He's a friend." He then went on to encourage Steve May, an openly gay Republican from Arizona, to run for office.

Moral Transformation in the Personal Struggle

Though there are awful people out there, the number one threat to gays is not from outside forces like Pat Robertson, Jerry Falwell, and other ministers of the far right. Rather, the greatest threat comes from the internal debate we each wage over shame, self-worth, and loneliness.

My friend Jason is twenty-two and works for CNN. Fresh out of college, he is typical of the next generation of gay men. I asked him what he thought about gay politics, and he responded, "Not much." When I asked him what issues are most important to his generation, he paused for a moment. "Well, employment laws and AIDS funding aren't really that relevant to me or my friends. Gay marriage and adoption are more relevant, but I guess what we really need are role models, values, and guidance. I don't see the gay community behaving like much of a community; just look how it treats unattractive people, for example. This sounds weird, but I often think I'd better find a boyfriend now, 'cause my looks are the best they're going to be, and in the future I'll have less value."

Jason's message may sound clichéd, but our fear of the values that prevail in the gay community has taken its toll on us. The greatest damage done by the religious right in America has been that in many cases it has succeeded, at a very deep level, in making gays feel bad about themselves, and, sadly, some in the gay community have taken that self-hatred and turned it on other gays and lesbians. The reality is that gays will never convince the society at large that we are good until *we* believe we are good and behave that way. We must first learn to love ourselves and believe that we too are children of God.

Brent Bozell, the head of the very conservative Media Research Center, was debating me on *Fox Morning News* in 1992 about the impact of gay bashing on the Republican Party's chances in the election; he was arguing that it had mobilized the base, while I argued that it would cost Bush the election. During the debate, Bozell had repeatedly made disparaging remarks about gays. I threw him a curve: "Brent, I find it odd that you are attacking gay Republicans, when your mentor and best friend was Terry Dolan, one of the most famous gay Republicans." He tightened up and responded mechanically: "Thank you for raising that. But you know as well as I know that Terry Dolan renounced his homosexuality and when activists like you came to seek his help, he told you to take a walk."

Terry Dolan had lived a double life, on the one hand working to build the conservative movement, and on the other being gay. As he came closer to death from AIDS, he lived a more openly gay lifestyle. But once he became very ill, his family moved in to forbid Terry from seeing his gay partner. In his final days he suffered under a fog of dementia. A priest was called in to obtain the confession or renunciation that Brent had spoken about. His partner and gay friends were kept away, and even had to hold a separate memorial service for him, as his parents refused to invite them to the family funeral. Terry's story and his questions of self-worth are not unusual, and have been repeated over and over again in the lives and deaths of gay men, most visibly as they have died untimely deaths from AIDS.

In his later years, Terry did try to find a way to support gay politics. Unfortunately, he found little trust among gay activists, and his time eventually ran out. The personal struggle of Dolan is more universal within the gay community than we'd like to acknowledge, and more often than not, the Church has not only not played the role of healer, it has played the role of harmer.

My friend Mark is a senior at Georgetown who struggled intensely to reconcile his homosexuality with his Catholicism. His goal always has been to be a priest. Over the last year, Mark reconciled his faith in God with his painful realization that the Church is only a human institution trying to understand God, and God created him as a gay man. When he finally developed enough confidence to take the next step, he told a priest he admired at Georgetown that he was gay. The priest's response in this very difficult moment was that Mark should stop taking communion—that he lived in sin. With stories like that, it is not hard to understand the abundance of self-hate and doubt in the gay world. To his credit, Mark's faith survived. Three months later he wrote an op-ed article in the Georgetown student newspaper condemning the university for its hostile environment for gay students. The next time he saw the priest from whom he had sought counsel, the priest walked past as if he wasn't there.

Spending a year questioning the values of his faith, Mark embarked on his new life in the gay world. He soon concluded that this world's most important value was looks.

"That's the rule of the game in the gay world," he observes. "I can either get a muscular body or live a lonely life. I don't want to be just a barfly my whole life, but if you want to meet someone, that's where you go."

★

A community that lost a generation to AIDS is in need of successful role models.

The most common spot for a gay getaway from Washington is Rehoboth Beach in Delaware. I accepted an invitation for a weekend in the sun, and sat at Poodle Beach—the gay beach—next to Mike, a friend I'd known for a couple of years through Log Cabin. Mike was the epitome of the ideal gay man, with hoop earrings in each ear, a handsome French Canadian face matched by an incredible body—big pecs and rock-hard abs—a Caesar haircut, and a dark tan; he looked every bit the part of a Greek god. His photo was in the local gay newspaper, modeling for a clothes store. When he got up to walk to the beach, a photographer stopped him to take his picture.

He works for a political consulting company in Washington during the week, but on weekends Mike sits at the center of the gay-circuit life—the epitome of the gay party scene. As I talked to Mike about gay politics and values, the veneer of the gay ideal melted away, and he spoke with an honesty that afforded incredible insight into the lives of many of us in the gay community.

I asked Mike what he believed should be the goal of gay politics, and he responded: "To be honest, I think we've pretty much got what we want. Most people don't care if you're gay. I mean, look at this beach full of openly success-ful gay men. I think most straights don't care."

I countered by naming prominent leaders of the reli-gious right and asked him, "Who is our worst enemy?" He hesitated before responding, "To be honest, our worst en-emy isn't the Christian Coalition, it's ourselves."

As the day progressed, more gay men gathered around the area where we were sitting, and I listened to the bitterness and viciousness of the conversation that followed. As each gay man made his way onto the beach, he was critiqued and ridiculed. "Look at that guy, he looks pregnant," one person commented, indicating an overweight man. "Does that guy own another bathing suit?" said another. Each comment was a typical reflection of how gay men too often treat one an-other. And the comments weren't for humor's sake; the men made them to tear down other gay men, in an effort to build up themselves. And each person in that group had to know that once he left the crowd, his faults and imperfections would be the topic of discussion.

As the crowd dispersed, I reviewed with Mike the com-ments of the crowd. With blunt honesty, Mike summed up what happened: "Sure these guys are vicious. Look, I'm Catholic, and the shame from my church and parents plays itself out. I think our low self-esteem makes us turn on each other, ya know, to rip each other apart."

Mike is popular in that crowd, but also is passionate about politics and doing good. I asked him how he strad-dles both worlds. "Well, our community has skewed values. I didn't make them, they just are what they are. If I want to be liked, I've got to be cute. And cute boys only want to sleep with other cute boys, so I've got to spend my time in the gym."

"So, is it simply about sex?" I asked him. "No," he responded, "truthfully it is still about being liked. Sex is great, but I find myself chasing certain popular guys to get them, and when I get them, I'm not interested. Because I just proved to myself that I'm attractive, that I'm okay."

We broke to get something to eat. Mike treated himself to a Popsicle and a bean burger. He prided himself on knowing the fat grams of each item. As he was about to eat the Popsicle, he saw on the label that it had eighteen grams of fat. "Enjoy yourself," I suggested. "No way. I'm just too much of a health nut," he responded as he threw the Popsicle away. I teased him about the health comment: "Come on, Mike, you don't value health. Last night you were doing drugs; today you're turning dark brown. This is about looks, and responding to the values that you described earlier."

We talked again about values. "We need a Martin Luther King to lead us," Mike concluded. "But as soon as anyone steps up as a leader, our community rips them apart." I mentioned Elizabeth Birch as a potential leader. "Look," Mike responded, "half the guys on this beach wouldn't know who Elizabeth Birch is, but they would know Jeff Stryker"—a porn star.

"You want to know who our leaders are?" Mike continued. "They're bartenders, club owners, club promoters, porn stars, and the circuit boys. I know I won't be cute much longer, and I don't know what I'll do when that happens. I'm valued in our community now because of my looks. Nobody really cares about me as a person. Everyone thinks I'm so popular, but the truth is I'm incredibly lonely. I just don't see anyone in our community valuing anything but superficial, empty things. You don't hear people saying, 'Wow, that guy volunteers for AIDS causes, I want to date him,' do you?"

So I asked him what his solution was. "I really don't know," Mike responded. "I think about this all of the time. Maybe you could get Congress to allow schools to help kids accept themselves. We just don't accept ourselves. Maybe therapy is the answer, but that's kind of like renting a friend. Eventually, you've got to believe in yourself, but I don't know how you do it. I'm smart, I can see what a dead end this lifestyle is, but I don't know any way out."

Late in the day, Mike pointed out a "ghost"—an old boyfriend he refused to speak with. I recommended to Mike that he make amends with the guy, whom he'd avoided for two years. "He's not worth even making up with. He's nothing," Mike concluded. "Try something different," I suggested. "Tell him you don't hold a grudge." After some badgering, Mike agreed to try this out. Later that night, Mike approached his ghost.

"Look, we don't need to avoid each other for the rest of our lives, do we?" Mike asked.

"I'm sorry for everything," his old boyfriend said in response.

"Were you just going to avoid me?"

"Actually, I was waiting all this time for you to talk to me."

★

The hunger for self-esteem and a firm set of personal values is one of the most common stories that I hear from gay friends in moments of honesty. Scott's story is another example. At twenty-eight, he already is the vice president of an advertising firm. He's got great looks, is incredibly smart, lives in the best neighborhood, and drives a Mercedes. He always spent his summers at Fire Island, the exclusive gay resort off New York's Long Island. But one summer he nearly had a breakdown.

"I was jogging down the beach, and I just started bawling. I couldn't stop crying, and finally, I just stopped running and sat by myself. I just realized that no matter how hard I tried to be liked in this crowd, I'd just never be cute enough or rich enough. I watch young gay guys socializing only with other fashionable, cute gay guys. Or older gay men with money who host parties or buy drugs to keep these boys around. I tried so hard to fit into that world, but it is all going nowhere. It's just people living self-destructive lives, doing drugs, drinking—and the sex is really the least of it, but it is totally a live-for-today mentality, because there's literally nothing there, nothing to it. We're all in a desperate search for purpose, for belonging, to finally be a part of the in crowd."

When I asked Scott about his values, he responded, "Well, I value true, loyal friends. People who like me for me. And I thought of every friend I had on the Island, and if I were in the hospital today dying, which ones of them would visit me. I realized I couldn't count on one person in this crowd."

I asked if he thought Fire Island was the problem. "No,"

he responded, "it is not the place, it is the person. We go to this fantasy island with no cars and no stores, to fill something empty inside us. We come here looking for something—to be liked, to find a boyfriend, to be seen as cool. The island is just the epitome of a place that plays out our insecurities."

His description of Fire Island is of a kind of never-never land where gay men suffer from the Peter Pan syndrome, thinking we never have to grow up. At times we are perpetually adolescent, fated to remain nervous twelve-year-olds with low self-esteem. We pump up our bodies to rid ourselves of the sissy label we all endured while growing up. We create the circuit-party in crowd to replace the in crowds in high school and the fraternities in college that rejected us, or that we had to lie about ourselves to join. It gives us the illusion that we belong, at least in a gay context. Sex, consumerism, drugs, and hedonism aren't themselves the problem, but often are symptoms of the deeper problem—our lack of self-acceptance and our failed efforts to find it through these valueless means is the root of it all.

When I followed up with Scott a year later, he'd found some peace with himself. I mockingly commented, "You better be careful, you'll be off the A list." "I'm on the C-minus list now," he responded with a laugh. "I just don't care anymore what that crowd thinks, and it is the most liberating thing that's ever happened to me. It's like when I first came out."

Personalizing the Political

Being a gay Republican has offered me a unique view of this world. As one acquaintance said, he'd like to invite me to a dinner party, but there would be others who simply wouldn't come if I was there, as they hate Republicans. Attacks on me in the gay community aren't over ideas—they're personal. In the summer of 1996, Tony Kushner, the playwright of *Angels in America*, in an *Advocate* op-ed piece described my efforts to work with the Dole-Kemp campaign at the Republican convention by saying that "he has crawled so far up his ass that he has disappeared." "Go back to divinity school," he implored me. "Go learn about social justice again." Barney Frank has for years enjoyed referring to the Log Cabin Republicans as "Uncle Tom's Cabin Club," saying we are simply apologists for the anti-gay right-wing Republicans.

The gay community reflects a severe lack of moral integrity when we demand that straight society accept us as different, and yet practice such severe forms of intolerance within our own community. The same viciousness found in the bars and on Poodle Beach plays out in politics.

There does seem to be a new move toward bridging this gap, and a desire to change all of this. For every slam I've taken in gay politics, there are those who believe in themselves enough to reach across. Vic Basile, a labor union Democrat, wrote the plan and helped raise the seed money to get Log Cabin's office off the ground. Andy Tobias, now the treasurer of the Democratic National Committee, helped raise the seed money to initially fund the office. Jeff Soref, a member of the Democratic National Committee, reached out to us and to the Giuliani administration to help gain passage of the city's comprehensive domestic partner law. Richard Socarides, in the most partisan of roles in the Democratic Party as the president's liaison to the gay community, reached out to the LCR so we could work together on nomination battles in those cases in which we shared a common concern. Brian Bond, former attack staffer at the DNC's gay and lesbian interests desk, now works with gay Republicans to support gay Republican candidates running for office.

Urvashi Vaid, the head of the National Gay and Lesbian Task Force's think tank, who disagrees with me on more issues than she agrees, has made such a point of reaching out to me that *Out* magazine's Michelangelo Signorile ran a story about us called "Opposites Attract." We must begin to model mutual respect and real understanding before we can ask the same of straight society. In the end, we may learn enough within our community to offer leadership to a society struggling to return the word "civil" to "civil society."

Another challenge for the gay politicos will be how we treat those of us who haven't yet made it out of the closet. Gay leaders have long called for gays to come out, as the first step toward our success. Integrity, honesty, and truthfulness would be required of each gay person. However, the honesty of those who are out doesn't afford them the right to become self-righteous about their brothers and sisters who haven't yet made the transition. Until we display compassion, understanding, and patience for our fellow gays and lesbians in the closet, we will miss the opportunity to lead in our culture's moral debate. They need role models who welcome them out and support them. They don't need our scorn; they deserve our empathy.

The agenda items for the gay movement are less important than the values we bring to these issues. The issues of civil debate such as employment laws, sodomy legislation repeal, or appropriate AIDS funding will pass away. They are already being replaced by other issues, such as gay marriage and creating families. But the need for gays to first love themselves and believe that, if no one else, God loves them must be the foundation of any true gay movement.

When I had scheduled a vacation in Boston to visit old friends, there was one I particularly needed to see. My friend Eduardo was dying of AIDS. In the 1980s Eduardo had been in the gay fast lane, but he found it personally unfulfilling. When he got involved in the 1990 state-level campaign of Mike Duffy, an openly gay Republican, it changed his life. He threw himself into political causes.

Doctors had predicted his death months earlier, and when I saw him for the first time in many months, I saw an old man who bore some vague resemblance to the Eduardo I knew. Each day I visited him that week, his old boyfriend and fellow members of the local Log Cabin Club, of which Eduardo was a member, stood vigil. But Eduardo didn't want to let go. "Mitt Romney [a former candidate for the U.S. Senate from Massachusetts] called me, did I tell you that?" He would keep reminding me of his love of politics.

His father and sister had arrived from his native

Venezuela to be with him. Eduardo had never resolved the gay issue with his family. His father was very uncomfortable, and Eduardo even on his deathbed held to the shame of being gay and having AIDS, constantly imploring me, "Don't talk about gay stuff in front of my dad."

His father didn't talk too much, but one afternoon he and I were eating lunch together. He had a *Time* magazine in his hands with a painting of Jesus on the cover and the headline "Miracles."

"Eduardo tells me you're a priest," he began with a thick accent, relying on Eduardo's sister to translate his Spanish when necessary. "Do you believe in miracles?" he added, pointing to the cover of the magazine.

"Yes," I responded.

"Because I believe that Eduardo is going to be healed through a miracle, if we all pray enough," he asserted.

I responded, "Sir, you and I are both Christians and so is Eduardo." He nodded. I continued, "The true miracle of our faith is the promise of eternal life, but Eduardo is hanging on to this life until he receives your blessing and understanding of who he is before he can go on to the next life."

He began to tear up and just looked down. Eduardo's sister told me later that that night he spoke with Eduardo and told him it was okay to let go. The following night was my last before heading back, and Eduardo and I prayed the Lord's Prayer together. I prayed in English, he in Spanish. A month later Eduardo passed to the next life, and I received a warm note from his sister saying how touched the family was by Eduardo's gay friends in Boston.

It occurred to me then that it was the Church's ignorance that helped drive a wedge between this father and son, and left Eduardo with feelings of shame in his death. It was the Church's ignorance that had Terry Dolan recanting his sexuality in a cloud of dementia on his deathbed. Sadly, the Church had chased so many gay people away from what they needed most of all—faith. And in so many of those situations, it was the gay friends and lovers who in a time of need showed their compassion in a way the Church only talks about. While the gay community tries to find values to guide our lives, we lead the society at large, which in this period of transition has begun that search as well.

When I lived in Massachusetts, I volunteered each Saturday to help run an outreach program in one of Boston's worst neighborhoods. And while many gays are adopting or having their own children, many more are mentors, teachers, and tutors. We've all heard the complaints from elder folks who resent paying school taxes because their kids are fully grown. Yet I've never heard a gay person complain about school taxes, when in many cities gays make up a sizable chunk of the school tax base. The gay community has values that we need to articulate more clearly both in the civic debate and to provide role models for our next generation.

Gay relationships are charting new waters that straights will soon have to navigate. With the new equality between men and women, straights are asking and answering the questions of how two people stay together through love, without the glue of children or economics. Gays and lesbians are pioneering relationships that hold together when both partners are equals. Gays and lesbians are delving into what it means to be an adult when you don't have children. We are trying to answer the question of whether monogamy is a more or a moral value. We are learning within our own very diverse community that we can get along. As our nation grows more diverse and identity politics grows obsolete, the success of the gay and lesbian community in respecting differences may be the most important value we can pass on to the greater society.

Our entire society is experiencing a vacuum of spiritual values, and that vacuum is being filled, unfortunately, by the only folks talking about values, those on the far right. The gay community has demonstrated time and again our values through our actions, but we have yet to articulate them, or to offer role models to the coming generation.

Seeing the Other Side

"What is your position on ordaining gays?" I asked the ordination council of the Philadelphia Baptist Association.

My decision to be ordained seemed to be preordained. I was named Richard for my great uncle, the Reverend Richard Tafel, pastor of the Swedenborgian Church at 22nd and Chestnut Streets in Philadelphia, and president of the Swedenborgian denomination. My middle name is the name of my grandfather, Leonard, who was the pastor of the Swedenborgian Church in Frankford, Philadelphia, and also onetime president of the church. The spiritual impact of these two great ministers' names seemed to send me down the track to ordination. As I grew older I learned of the familial connection to the great German martyr Dietrich Bonhoeffer, who became an instant hero to me.

Odd as it was, I loved Sunday School, where by fourth grade I had memorized the books of the Bible. I was asking questions of my Sunday School teachers that they would have to refer to the pastor. I found Sunday services, on the other hand, boring, especially communion Sundays. Fortunately, my very secular German soccer club held its games on Sundays. So I would go to Sunday School and leave church with my soccer uniform under my dress suit.

My father was determined that if I missed church for soccer, our rides to the game would require theological discussion. Though a successful businessman, my father has a wide knowledge of theology. We would have deep discussions on Swedenborg, the Trinity, life after death, and salvation. These were much more valuable than any church service I ever attended. In all of his discussions, he would stress the Swedenborgian message, that earthly life is temporal and we must live life for the eternal. We should not be overly worried about life on earth, but much more concerned with our eternal life, which begins now.

While at the Baptist Church we always heard about who was and who wasn't getting into heaven, my father gave me theological insights from beyond. The theologian Swedenborg had been given a view of heavenly life, and his view of heaven was incredible. Swedenborg's insights took me well beyond the childlike faith so many in the evangelical church had.

With my love of theology well established as I entered puberty, I began to realize that I was gay. I didn't know anyone who was gay; I had no role models, either in life or on TV. Homosexuality, it was explained to me, was the product of young boys being forced to wear women's clothes or not having any male role models. Yet I had three brothers, two sisters, and plenty of male role models. When the topic was raised at a youth meeting, we all snickered and were told to read the story of Sodom—enough said.

And so I prayed, and prayed, waiting for the Holy Spirit to rid my body of homosexual desire the way I'd seen televangelists apparently rid people of wretched diseases. I got no response. The pressure of my religious upbringing and the clear fact that I was attracted to men were doomed for a collision. I sought counsel from respected adults, using the roundabout way of asking about someone I knew. I remember every anti-gay comment I ever heard while growing up, particularly the remark of one friend who said, "They should all be taken out and shot."

More than once, I thought that it would be easier to be dead than to be a homosexual. I continued to pray, for if I was gay, it was more than just a change in lifestyle—it would mean the end of my lifetime dream of entering the ministry. In the midst of that confusion and turmoil, I finally did hear the still, small voice of God. It told me the last thing I expected to hear; it said that He had created all things good, and that I was good, and that God loved me no matter what the world did or thought. While this moment should have given me peace, and did, it was also frightening because I knew very well the discrimination, hatred, and disapproval I would encounter from family, friends, and the society at large. It is both frightening and exhilarating to put your life in God's hands, and that's what I knew I was about to do. This transcendent experience of the divine presence remains the foundation for all that I do. True spirituality had to reach through the noise of the Church to touch my heart.

When I arrived at Harvard Divinity School to begin my Master of Divinity degree in 1984, I was also coming out as a gay man. It seemed clear to me that ordination wasn't a possibility, so what was I going to do? Did I belong at Harvard at all? Because of my Swedenborgian background, I was always looking for some spiritual sign that I was on the right track.

Upon arriving in Cambridge for the first time, I immediately went to the location of the Swedenborg School of Religion outside Harvard Square. My grandmother had told me many stories of her life with my grandfather, living at the school in the 1920s. Instead, I found that the Harvard Gund School of Design had replaced it, and all that remained was the beautiful Swedenborgian Chapel, under the ministry of a cousin of mine.

A few months later, I became the seminarian at Harvard's Memorial Church. I was offered the position of running the summer services and, knowing I was short on money, the church offered the opportunity to work in Sparks House, the home of Peter Gomes, Professor of Christian Morals and Pusey Minister in the Memorial Church.

A short time after I began working there, he exclaimed, upon hearing about my Swedenborgian connection, "Well, you're living in the old Swedenborg School of Religion! They moved the building in the 1960s. You're living in the same place that your grandparents lived sixty years earlier." That was exactly the type of spiritual sign I needed to show me that I was going down the right path, wherever it took me.

Three years later, I asked, "What is your position on ordaining gays?"

My question was met with a stunned silence, a few raised eyebrows, and a genuine look of concern from my hometown pastor. I was about to graduate from Harvard Divinity School in the spring of 1987, and was meeting with the leaders of the Philadelphia Baptist Association to pass the first denominational hurdle toward ordination.

Several things were required: I would have to graduate with a Master of Divinity degree from a reputable seminary or divinity school. Next, I would need to be approved by the American Baptist leadership in the Philadelphia Association. Third, I would need to be "called" by a church for the ordination to take place. Finally, and most difficult, I would need to be voted in through an ordination council, which would bring together two members of each church in my association for a theological question-and-answer period, followed by a vote.

Upon graduation, Peter Gomes offered me a full-time position in the church, which would serve as my "call." On spiritual matters, there was no one I respected more, and he was adamant in encouraging me to be ordained, even though I was gay. We spoke about the prophetic voice within the church, which only centuries later is appreciated and vindicated.

So there I was with the church leaders, asking them about their position on the ordination of gays. They proceeded by answering that the denomination didn't ordain *open* homosexuals. This meant I was confronted with the ultimate hypocritical position toward homosexuality that permeates American society, in which if you don't tell me, it is okay, even if you are—"don't ask, don't tell."

I decided to play this game during the ordination process, under one ground rule—if asked, I would never lie about being gay, and it was sure to come up. The panel of well-educated and theologically liberal church leaders proceeded to ask me questions on my theological paper. They were impressed with my Harvard experience, but were disappointed that I hadn't properly learned to use "inclusive" language in my reference to God, meaning gender-neutral language, which was a product of feminist theology and a litmus test for cutting-edge, progressive theologians. I had referred to Him as God the Father.

After passing that review, and following my graduation from divinity school, my home church in Churchville, Pennsylvania, hosted my ordination council. Two by two, like the animals on the Ark, the delegates came in, each carrying a Bible.

The moderator for the proceedings pointed out that my council had the largest attendance of any he had seen. Slightly paranoid about the gay issue, I asked if he knew why. "Because you graduated from godless Harvard," he responded. Each person was given a copy of my theological statement, which I then read aloud, and the questions began immediately.

After the first few questions, I knew I was in trouble. No, I didn't believe Adam was a real person—strike one. I couldn't say for sure who does or doesn't get into heaven, that's up to God—strike two. This question of who is saved dominated the entire discussion. I knew that they wanted me to condemn those secular folks who don't go to church. One questioner asked, if John 3:16 says, "For God so loved the world that He gave His only begotten Son, that whoever believes in Him should not perish but have everlasting life," then doesn't that tell us that only born-again Christians are saved?

My years of Bible baseball had taught me too well. I asked about his interpretation of John 3:17. The questioner looked puzzled. Bible-believing Christians were usually good at memorizing selected verses, not paragraphs. I responded, "The next verse tells us that God came into the world to redeem it, not to condemn it. If God doesn't come to condemn, then who are we sinful people to believe we can go around condemning others? In fact, the gospel of Jesus Christ was about forgiveness and compassion. I'll leave judging another's salvation to God."

This statement only further angered the fundamentalist types in the audience. The next questioner asked, "Hypothetically, could a person who lives in America and hears the word of God, but still rejects Him, get into heaven?" I responded, "I don't believe it is my job as a Christian to engage in hypothetical or any judgment of another's salvation." Sad to say, much of the Church's time is spent deciding who is in and who is out, justifying the Church's own belief.

I was clearly losing the battle. My family stayed away that night, probably fearful that I would make some proclamation about being gay. The front row of the church was filled with the wonderful old ladies from my church who had known me since I was a child. They had come to support me and to host the social afterward. They seemed perplexed by my answers. They appeared to be thinking to themselves, "I never knew he believed that." My panicking pastor, with a heart of gold, was more explicit. He passed me a note: "Stress your personal relationship with Jesus Christ!" I smiled back at him, but I wasn't going to play that game either.

My theology was clearly too liberal for this audience. After refusing to condemn Jews to hell or acknowledge the existence of the Garden of Eden, I was asked whether I believed the story of Creation. I asked, Which one, Genesis 1 or 2? They grew more upset. Another questioner cut to the chase: "Do you take the Bible literally?" I answered, "The Bible was my source of guidance and spiritual knowledge, but not an idol whose every word I worshipped. No, I don't take the Bible literally. And we must all be careful not to worship idols."

That was it. A gasp sounded somewhere in the church. Again, I find my life a bit of a paradox. Here I was, the same person who had been considered a right-winger at Harvard, but among this crowd I was about as liberal as anyone they had ever seen. One of the ladies in the front row began to sniffle. I was in trouble, and yet I felt an abiding peace that I can describe only as the peace that surpasses all understanding.

After three hours of questioning—what seemed like an eternity—I was asked to leave the room for the vote. My pastor had turned white. We both knew that my ordination didn't look good. "You should have stressed your personal relationship with Jesus," he mumbled under his breath.

I waited for the vote, and when my pastor returned to bring me back out, he looked sick. "They want to ask you more questions before they vote," he told me. I returned to a very angry and exhausted group. They notified me that some delegates wanted to hear my position on a few social issues before they voted. I had been waiting for this.

The first questioner asked, "Do you support the ordination of women?" "Yes, I support our church's position on this"—strike one, for even though it was "accepted" in this church, it remained a divisive issue to many. Next question: "Do you support abortion in any circumstance?" "Yes, in certain circumstances," I responded. I was tired after three hours of questions and had become more direct. Then came the big one: "If a homosexual came to you for counseling, first, would you welcome him for counseling? And second, if you did, would you condemn him?"

In that moment it was clear to me that if I answered, "Yes, I would condemn the homosexual," I might still be ordained. But the verse "For what will it profit a man if he gains the whole world, and loses his own soul?" was ringing in my head. I began my answer coyly: "First, I would counsel anyone who sought my help. Second, I don't know if I'd condemn the homosexual, unless I knew what he'd done. For example, if he murdered someone or stole something, I'd condemn those acts."

That was it. They had had enough of my rope-a-dope.

My questioner screamed back, *"I mean simply for being a homosexual! Would you condemn him?"*

I feigned being puzzled, as if I couldn't even imagine such a question, and responded, "For being gay? No."

He exploded, screaming, *"What does the Bible say? What does the Bible say?"* I lost my cool too, and yelled back, "I'll take you verse for verse on what the Bible says! Let's go through it *right now!*" A shriek came from one of the old women in the first row. My pastor just hung his head. The moderator jumped up in front of me and yelled, "We won't treat candidates this way!"

"Forget the question," my inquisitor responded, "we've heard enough. I make a motion we vote on the candidate now." A second followed, and I was escorted to the pastor's study again. I laughed with God, saying, "If you want me to be ordained, it will take nothing less than a miracle. It won't happen through the votes out there." I was completely at peace.

After a few moments, the pastor opened the study door with a big grin.

"You won, congratulations."

I was shocked, hardly accepting the news as I was escorted back to the sanctuary. The ladies in the front row and the audience greeted me with applause. The fundamentalists, very publicly and rudely, stormed out. People whispered that I had won by a slim majority. But who voted for me? I wondered.

A greeting line to the social formed. The church ladies were smiling ear to ear, sharing with one another their earlier fears. I noticed a trend in my well-wishers. The older ones were the most supportive. One older gentleman introduced himself as Lincoln (I immediately drew the connection) and told me, "I've been to more ordination councils than you are years old. In all my years, I've never seen a more honest candidate.

"You knew the answers that they wanted to hear, but you stuck to your beliefs. That's the leadership our faith so desperately needs. The Lord has an incredible vision for your future. And, by the way, I didn't agree with a darn thing you said about Adam and hell or any of that stuff," he added, smiling.

In January 1988, I was ordained in a service in that very church. Peter Gomes dazzled the congregation, and the family and friends who attended, with his sermon. Three years later, Peter would come out as a gay man himself in response to an anti-gay Christian magazine on campus. He went on to write *The Good Book: Reading the Bible with Mind and Heart* in 1996, a major best-seller.

★

My ordination story reflects the paradox that the greatest inhibitor of God reaching gay people in America today is, sadly, the Church. In my ordination council, at no time was I quizzed about the teachings of Jesus, His challenge of compassion, humility, and forgiveness. Like the religious right of His time, the Pharisees, my questioners wanted to be assured that they were better than others, and others were worse than them. Their own low view of themselves was reflected in their theology that scapegoats others in an effort to make themselves feel better. The enduring teachings of Jesus—honesty, love, forgiveness, compassion, and a life of self-examination—however, seemed upheld in the words of "Lincoln" and in the hearts of the women in the front row.

What strikes me as most amazing in my ordination is the power of God. The only way anyone can explain how I got ordained that night must be by acknowledging a force greater than any in the room. Despite the Church's shortcomings, God had reached into that church that night and, I believe, worked through His people. They voted for me in spite of their beliefs in theological positions; they voted their hearts. I believe that ultimately this is exactly how gays will achieve the fair treatment they deserve—through a spiritual force that works in spite of our human limitations.

After what I, a deeply religious believer, went through in an effort to serve the Church, it is no surprise to me that a majority of gays have felt abandoned by the Church. A friend in my old church told me recently that she had heard some new church members suggest that my ordination be revoked because of my political work in the Log Cabin Republicans. At moments like that I think of a line in a 1932 letter from Dietrich Bonhoeffer to my father's cousins in suburban Philadelphia with whom he stayed during his visit to America: "I enjoy my calling too, though each day it is becoming more clear to me how hard it is to be a true minister."

The success of gays as a social group in America is a

story of paradoxes. The emergence of our group identity was a paradox: we were brought together by socialists because of the new liberties that our free market democracy made possible. Another paradox is that gays will win the struggle against those who claim to speak for morality in our society, but only when we do a better job of articulating the morality of our cause. We must remind society that our cause is fundamentally about people being honest. We must show them that our cause is about people who want to love each other, that we fight for so many who live in the shadows and closets of fear, and that, in the end, we are fighting another battle for people so that they can have the freedom to be different. If we succeed in doing that, then political parties that have made a strategy of shunning us will seek our support.

There will be periods of backlash and major setbacks for us, but we are riding a wave into the information society, which will only speed up our successes, to the day when people will have to really think hard to remember when gays and lesbians weren't accepted as part of the fabric of our country.

Our legacy is a paradox too. Gays have been persecuted most viciously by those claiming to be protectors of society's most treasured relationships, family and marriage, yet we might be able to offer new models of important relationships to members of straight society grappling with feelings of isolation and loneliness. We are hated by those who speak of values, and yet we can be role models of values by showing how we all should treat one another.

The ultimate paradox is that gay people will be liberated by the same spiritual forces and values that so many gays believe can only oppress them. Now is the time for gays to get beyond our rejection reactions, to develop principles that will guide us in the civic arena and a faith that will guide us beyond politics to how we will live our lives with faith, hope, and love.

INDEX

INDEX